How to Retire Happy

How to Retire Happy

The 12 Most Important Decisions You Must Make Before You Retire

Fourth Edition
Fully Revised and Updated

STAN HINDEN

New York   Chicago   San Francisco   Lisbon   London
Madrid   Mexico City   Milan   New Delhi
San Juan   Seoul   Singapore   Sydney   Toronto

The *McGraw·Hill* Companies

4 5 6 7 8 9 0   QFR/QFR   1 8 7 6 5 4 3

ISBN   978-0-07-180069-3
MHID   0-07-180069-7

e-ISBN   978-0-07-180070-9
e-MHID   0-07-180070-0

McGraw-Hill books are available at special quantity discounts to use as premiums and sales promotions or for use in corporate training programs. To contact a representative, please e-mail us at bulksales@mcgraw-hill.com.

This book is printed on acid-free paper.

Library of Congress Cataloging-in-Publication Data

Hinden, Stan.
  How to retire happy : the 12 most important decisions you must make before you retire / by Stan Hinden. — Fourth Edition.
      pages cm
  Includes index.
  ISBN-13: 978-0-07-180069-3 (alk. paper)
  ISBN-10: 0-07-180069-7 (alk. paper)
  1. Retirement—United States—Planning.   2. Retirement income—United States.
  3. Retirement—Economic aspects—United States.   I. Title.
  HQ1063.2.U6H56 2012
  646.7'90973—dc23

                                                                          2012039679

For Sara,
who made the journey with me

Contents

Contents

Foreword

Congratulations! You are about to read the splendid new edition of a wonderful, sensible, and simple book that will be a priceless asset to you. If you're thinking about retiring, have decided to retire within the next several years, or have decided not to retire just yet—or even if you retired some years ago—Stan Hinden's book will help you analyze the 12 vital decisions you must make at retirement and offer expert advice in each area—and do so in words that are easy to read, bereft of financial jargon and gobbledygook.

I happen to be in the category "not ready to retire." While I'm chronologically 83 years of age, if you measure by the age of the heart that was transplanted into my chest some 17 years ago, I'm a mere child of 43. I love my work too much to stop just yet. But I've already personally considered many of the decisions that Stan discusses, and I will be that much better prepared when (and if!) I finally decide to retire.

Most of my own expertise, such as it may be, is in the world of finance. My entire six-decade-plus career has been in the mutual fund industry, and I fully endorse just about every one of Stan Hinden's recommendations about investing for, and in, retirement. To be able to afford a comfortable retirement, for example, importantly depends on the power of time and the magic of long-term compounding of investment returns, all the while sidestepping the tyranny of compounding excessive investment costs. Almost invariably, such a strategy is best implemented by using cost-efficient, tax-efficient index funds, a breed that is at last getting the widespread acceptance that it merits.

Income in Retirement

For most families, Social Security is a critical part of retirement income. Although we can't control the schedule of benefits, we can control the time when our payments begin. The advice this book gives is good: the longer you wait (up to age 70), the larger the check you'll receive thereafter. While Social Security is designed to provide a minimal standard for retirement income, its stream of benefits can be estimated to have a capital value of some $300,000 at age 70. That value is even better than it looks, for it is the equivalent of a fixed-income investment with a built-in hedge against inflation—two priceless assets when you retire.

Stan Hinden's book is also right on the mark in its chapters on making decisions about company pensions, 401(k) corporate thrift plans, and individual retirement accounts. His advice benefits greatly from his firsthand experience (some derived from his own investment mistakes) as he presents important information on investing during retirement—virtually all of which I heartily endorse. His five "Golden Rules" are, well, golden. Yet they are so simple and basic that too many investors pay no attention to them and suffer the consequences.

His advice on asset allocation and the need for significant holdings in bonds or annuities to produce income is also well worth heeding. That advice may have seemed too cautious in 2000 when the first edition of this book was published, right after the greatest bull market in history. But now, after two stock market crashes (in 2000–2002 and again in 2007–2009), the advice seems almost prescient.

Indeed, the kind of balanced approach to investing that Stan recommends has performed admirably in the 11 years since I wrote the foreword to the first edition of *How to Retire Happy* in August 2000. For example, a $10,000 investment in Vanguard Wellington Fund—a conservative balanced fund with about 65 percent of its assets in stocks and 35 percent in bonds—would have provided an average annual return of 7 percent per year. That is, by August 2012, it would have grown to $22,500, assuming that all dividends were reinvested. While many investors complain about returns in "the lost decade," that outcome seems remarkably satisfactory.

Investing Today

Alas, I must caution you that such a generous return is unlikely to recur in the coming decade. Current conditions in the financial markets are more challenging. In the bond market, the yield on the 10-year U.S. Treasury note has plummeted from 6 percent to just 1.6 percent, suggesting a reduction of some 70 percent(!) in bond returns during the years ahead. Some enhancement in return could be achieved by placing greater emphasis on an investment-grade corporate bond index fund, which now yields about 3 percent. There is, of course, some extra credit risk involved, and you should carefully consider this before you take action.

In the stock market, on the other hand, conditions appear to be somewhat more favorable. The dividend yield has doubled from 1 percent to 2 percent, and market valuations seem to have returned to sanity. Stocks were selling at a speculative multiple of

30 times earnings in 2001; today's multiple of 16 times is pretty much in line with historical norms. But risk abounds. The wise retirement-plan investor will not reach out too far for income. Stan's advice on asset allocation comes to the same conclusion: be careful!

Other Issues

Stan Hinden recognizes that a successful retirement requires much more than a successful investment program. His chapters on health insurance, preparing for illness, deciding where you want to live, and estate planning present a wide variety of ideas, many of which I had never given much consideration. But I'm considering them now. And in his final chapter—on successful aging—he gives all of us in the sixties, seventies, and eighties age group a marvelous compendium of good advice, including how to maintain our physical and mental energies, some tricks we can use when memory fails (yes, it happens to me, too), and how to remain actively engaged in the great game of life. Of course, meeting that challenge remains elusive for all of us—even for Stan himself. He touches on the changes he made in his own plans when his wife developed Alzheimer's disease several years ago.

This is a great book because it fills a major gap in the investment literature. There are countless books about accumulating financial assets for retirement, but there are few about what to do when you get there, and Stan's book offers as intelligent and comprehensive an approach as I've seen. It takes a great deal of the mystery and confusion out of retirement and, by so doing, allays much of the anxiety you may feel as the time approaches.

To say that Stan Hinden is well qualified to write a book on retirement is something like saying that Tiger Woods is well qualified to hold a golf clinic. First, as the saying goes, Stan has "been there, done that." He's closed out his remarkable career as a successful journalist, retiring from his job as a financial columnist for the *Washington Post* in 1996, and now has 16 years of retirement under his belt. Although he's remained active and productive, obviously investing a large amount of time in writing this book ("having it both ways," as the author puts it), he knows where the challenges and opportunities lie.

With his firsthand expertise on retirement, his journalist's gift for simple writing, and his considerable financial expertise, Stan Hinden has carried off with considerable success the challenge of helping those of us who are considering or experiencing retirement. In *How to Retire Happy: The 12 Most Important Decisions You Must Make Before You Retire*, he has done so with flair and common sense. I am confident that his wisdom will improve your own preparation for retirement, and help all of us who take the opportunity this book presents to consider his helpful and constructive advice.

John C. Bogle
Founder and former Chief Executive
The Vanguard Group
Valley Forge, Pennsylvania
August 29, 2012

Preface

This is the book I wish I had been able to read before I retired. If I had, my monthly Social Security check would be fatter, my company pension would be better, my retirement savings account would be significantly larger, and I'd have a better chance of making my money last during what I hope will be a long retirement.

But that's not all. If I had known then what I know now, I would have been better prepared, both psychologically and emotionally, for my retirement. I also would have had a keener appreciation for the life-enhancing opportunities and experiences that retirement can bring you.

I retired from the *Washington Post* in 1996. I was then 69 years old, and I had spent 23 years at the *Post*—the last 12 years as a financial columnist, writing about stocks and mutual funds. All told, I spent about 45 years in journalism as a reporter, writer, and editor.

Several months after I retired, I began writing a column for the *Post* called "Retirement Journal" that chronicled my experiences as a retiree. In essence, this book is the story of my retirement: what I learned and what I think you should know about the subject. My goal is to take the mystery out of retirement and to reduce the confusion that many retirees feel.

Shortly after I left my full-time job, I realized that I was woefully unprepared to make many of the decisions that are required of a retiree. I knew little, if anything, about Social Security, Medicare, Medigap, Medicare HMOs, long-term care, mandatory IRA withdrawals, pensions, and so on. But even though I was uninformed, I had to make far-reaching personal decisions on all of those subjects. Inevitably, as you will read, I made some bad decisions and learned some costly lessons.

The job of writing a regular column about my retirement experiences opened a window for me on a part of life that I had not known much about or even thought much about. Indeed, the more I learned, the more convinced I became that preparation and knowledge are the keys to a happy retirement.

It has been said that retirement is not an event but a process. If so, that process should begin long before you turn in your retirement papers. It is simply not logical to expect that you can learn everything you need to know to make major retirement decisions in a few days or even a few weeks, as I tried to do.

So consider this book to be a reporter's firsthand report from the front lines of retirement. My hope is that this easy-reader tour will help future retirees better prepare for the day when they stop working full-time. I also hope the book will help current retirees find ways to improve their retirement experiences.

Retirement in America was once a casual, even drab, "You're over the hill" experience. It was a sign that the retiree was nearing the end of his productive life and was even getting close to the end of life itself.

Today, retirement in America has changed dramatically. It has become an upbeat, full-speed-ahead, "Let's start a second career" experience, made possible by longer life spans, tax-deferred savings plans, and government-sponsored income and health programs.

How to Retire Happy has 12 chapters, each dealing with one of the 12 key decisions that retirees must make during the retirement process.

Some of the decisions are related to our attitudes toward life and work and the complex emotions that surround retirement. We are faced with many questions: how we feel about leaving our longtime friends and colleagues at work, how we feel about relocating to a new community, and even how we feel about growing older.

Some of our other decisions involve the web of government programs and regulations that affect all retirees. They include the age at which we take our Social Security payments, the way we manage our healthcare, and even how we make our mandatory IRA withdrawals when we reach age 70½. You don't have to be a rocket scientist to figure out your withdrawals—although it would help.

Finally, there are the financial decisions that will determine whether you will have a comfortable or an uncomfortable retirement. I often think about that old saying, "I've been rich, and I've been poor. Rich is better." Smart saving and investing can make the difference. But as the book points out, you will have to work at it.

Retirement is not a simple matter. But your retirement decisions will be a lot easier if you take the time to understand your choices. Then you can start having fun. A happy retirement is within everybody's reach. The time to start is now. The place to start is here.

An Update on the Author and His Wife

As you will soon discover, *How to Retire Happy* is, in many ways, the story of both my retirement and that of my wife, Sara. We were married in 1953, and in May of 2012, as the fourth edition of this book was being prepared, we marked our fifty-ninth wedding anniversary. The event was not quite as joyous as it might have been because by then, Sara was suffering from Alzheimer's disease. As a result, she now lives in a small group home for dementia patients, where she receives 24-hour care. Sara is also afflicted by aphasia, a condition that prevents her from expressing coherent thoughts.

Signs of Sara's illness first appeared in 2007, when she was 78, and the diagnosis of Alzheimer's disease soon followed. Slowly but steadily, she lost her cognitive abilities. She moved to the group home in 2011 when she was no longer able to perform basic functions of daily living.

Needless to say, Sara's condition dramatically changed both her retirement and mine. Until then, we had been poster children for a happy, upbeat retirement. When I delivered a talk about retirement, members of the audience would often crowd around Sara to question her about her own experiences with retirement.

I am discussing Sara's illness at the start of this new edition because my experience with Alzheimer's disease has given me a new perspective on how one prepares for serious illness during retirement. I plan to share those thoughts with you in Decisions 8 and 9, the health-related chapters.

For many retirees, as they age, death and disease are unwelcome realities of life. But for those who remain healthy, the challenge is to find purpose and happiness in retirement. It can be done. Some suggestions will be found in Decision 12, "How Can I Age Successfully?"

Stan Hinden

Acknowledgments

My thanks go first to David Ignatius, who was the assistant managing editor/business at the *Washington Post* in 1996, when I retired from my job as a financial columnist. It was at his suggestion that I began to write a new column called "Retirement Journal," a first-person report on my experiences as a retiree. His encouragement and support were crucial to the success of the column, which led to this book. I also had wonderful support for my column from the executives, editors, and writers at the *Post*.

The key to any successful journey is having a good guide to show you the sights. On my journey through the land of retirement, I have had many excellent guides.

At the Social Security Administration, my guides for this edition included Senior Public Affairs Specialist Dorothy J. Clark, who gave freely of her time and knowledge as she helped me update the chapter on Social Security.

My guide through the jungle of estate planning was attorney Rhonda J. Macdonald. I am grateful for her infinite patience and meticulous attention to detail.

I had help finding my way through the maze called "required minimum distributions"—the money you must take out of your IRA accounts—from Christine S. Fahlund, vice president and senior financial planner, T. Rowe Price Investment Services, and Neil Cooper, senior financial planning analyst, T. Rowe Price Investment Services.

My guide through the complex area of health insurance was L. Sue Andersen, a member of the Provider Reimbursement Review Board, Centers for Medicare and Medicaid Services (CMS). Her expertise was invaluable. My sincere thanks also go to Melissa Gannon, vice president, insurance and bank ratings, at TheStreet.com Ratings, Inc., for her help with Medigap statistics.

My thanks also go to Paul E. Forte, chief executive officer of Long Term Care Partners, LLC, for his insights and expertise in the field of long-term care.

I am especially grateful for the encouragement that this edition received from Mary E. Glenn, editorial director, business, at McGraw-Hill Professional.

My deepest thanks go to my friend and researcher Pat Kloehn, who worked tirelessly to help organize and edit the fourth edition of this book.

My sons and their wives, Alan and Gina Hinden and Lawrence and Denice Rothman Hinden, and my daughter, Pamela S. Hinden, continue to hearten me with their enthusiasm for my writings and their endless patience with my efforts to find my way through an electronic world.

How to Retire Happy

Am I Ready to Retire?

Are You Ready to Retire?

When the stress levels at work seem unbearable, it's easy to be flippant and shout, "You bet I'm ready to retire. Let me out of here!"

At such moments, it's also easy to fantasize about all the things you could do if you didn't have to go to work every day. You can see yourself soaking up the sun on a tropical beach, whiling away the hours on a golf course, or having gobs of time to read, watch movies, or trade stocks online.

You think about all the things you've wanted to do but never had time for: cruising around the Greek islands, touring Australia and New Zealand, watching the bullfights in Spain, or enjoying Carnaval in Brazil.

And then you suddenly realize that you could even buy a season ticket for your local baseball team and go to games in the middle of the week! What a luxury!

It's also quite wonderful to think about all the things you could give up: all your bosses, all those memos, and all those boring meetings. Gone, too, from your life would be those rush-hour traffic jams and the frustrations of your daily commute. If your job requires you to travel, you could stop bouncing around in airplanes and trying to sleep on lumpy hotel-room pillows.

As a retired person, you'd be free to make your own schedule: to do what you want to do and go where you want to go when you want to go there. Ah, freedom!

But wait! Remember the old adage: if it sounds too good to be true, it probably is. Like a lot of daydreams, these visions of retirement may or may not be realistic. They may not even be what you really want when you retire.

The fact is that when you face the question, "Am I ready to retire?" your answer may have little to do with your fantasies and a lot more to do with your age, your health, your family, the nature of your job, your financial situation, and your outlook on life.

So to be realistic, let's look at the pros and cons of retiring. We'll discuss three good reasons for retiring and three equally good reasons for not retiring.

Then we'll talk about people who have it both ways: they retire and—guess what?—then go back to work, usually part-time. As people live longer and healthier lives, the part-time option is becoming more and more popular.

We'll also look at what life is like for married couples after they retire. And we'll talk about the psychological impact of retirement—how you can go from a busy, even frantic, working life to a laid-back but productive retirement.

Three Good Reasons for Retiring

REASON 1: THE TIME IS RIGHT

If there is "a time under the sun for everything," then surely there will be a time in your life when you can look in the mirror and rightfully tell yourself, "I've worked hard all my life. I've met every challenge life has thrown at me. It's time for me to stop working and to start living life my own way. These are the years that belong to me."

If this is how you truly feel, that's fine. Once you retire, you'll be free to shape your life in the manner that gives you the greatest satisfaction and happiness. But to make the most of your new freedom, you'll need a plan.

In a way, retiring is like going on a trip abroad. You wouldn't just pack a suitcase and board a plane. You'd try to prepare for your journey. You'd read guidebooks about the places you plan to visit, study currency exchange rates, and find out what kind of weather to expect. And, of course, you'd prepare an itinerary so that you'd know where you were going and when.

Similarly, if you want your journey into retirement to be successful, you must do two things. First, you need to equip yourself with the information you'll need on your journey into the world of Social Security, Medicare, Medigap, long-term-care insurance, pensions, and 401(k) plans. Second, you need to decide what you want to do in retirement.

Doing nothing is not a viable option for most people. Studies show that people who retire from active careers and become couch potatoes often suffer from depression and other ills associated with feeling useless and unwanted.

Your retirement plan can take many forms. You can spend your time improving your golf or tennis game, coaching a kids' soccer or baseball team, working for a service club such as the

Lions or Kiwanis, or volunteering for a charitable or community organization. Many retirees enjoy spending time with their children and grandchildren. I know I do.

Retirement is a great time to complete some of your long-delayed personal projects. You may want to take some college courses, learn to play a musical instrument, or try your hand at writing mystery novels or painting. Many retirees—even those starting at late ages—demonstrate unusual creativity and artistic skills.

Whatever you decide to do in retirement, your plan should have one main objective: to keep you mentally and physically active and in close contact with other people. That is the way to achieve a successful retirement.

REASON 2: YOU HAVE MORE COMPELLING THINGS TO DO

As we age and gain experience, we often find that our goals in life become clearer. So it was with my friend Jane Hoden. Religion, faith, and community service had long been the cornerstones of her life. Inwardly, she knew that when she retired someday, she would find a way to fulfill her personal commitment to be of service to others.

"I believe God has a plan for our lives, which is revealed in time," Jane says.

"In 1999," Jane recalled, "my mother lived with us. It gave us great insight into what life is like for a person who is elderly, has significant health and financial issues, and feels that life is not within [her] control."

Jane said she soon realized that while churches focus on the needs of youth, the newly married, and active adults, they rarely address the needs of seniors. The more Jane studied the problem, the more she became convinced that forming a ministry for seniors was destined to be her calling in retirement.

In 2001, Jane, who was then 55, retired from the federal government, where she had worked for 31 years as a public information specialist and as the manager of the news division in her agency. Her government pension was reduced somewhat because she took "early retirement," but she didn't believe money would be a problem. Her husband, Paul, was a retired Air Force colonel with his own pension.

"We looked at his income and my income in retirement, at our savings and our expenses, and we decided we could afford to retire," Jane said.

To enjoy an active retirement and pursue Jane's ministry for seniors, the couple moved to Virginia Beach, Virginia, where they became co-leaders of the Senior Adult Ministry at Spring Branch Community Church. The programs, Jane said, are designed for people 50 and older and are intended to help "retirees who need a connection to people who will provide support and caring." Jane believed that she and other volunteers would be able to brighten the lives of many seniors who were lonely and isolated.

Retiring at 55 was "a golden opportunity," she said.

And so it seemed until 2006, when Jane's dream was interrupted by a diagnosis of breast cancer. Three surgeries were followed by months of chemotherapy and radiation and by some deep reflection about what she wanted out of life. In November 2007, the Hodens left Virginia Beach for Fort Myers, Florida, where they bought an apartment at the Shell Point Retirement Community. Shell Point is a continuing-care retirement community (CCRC) where Jane will have whatever assisted living or nursing care she might need in the future.

Jane's reflections on the course of her life led to a decision to devote more time to personal pursuits, including photography and travel. "There are times," she said, "when you have to look into yourself and decide what makes you happy."

One thing that makes Jane and Paul especially happy is their regular fellowship, prayer, and Bible study meeting with other Shell Point residents, an activity sponsored by the Sanibel Community Church on nearby Sanibel Island. Jane, who is 67, has been cancer-free for five years, an important milestone for cancer patients. With her health stable, she and Paul have been touring the United States in an RV. "Each year from May through September," Jane said, "we escape Florida's heat and hurricanes and head for the open road. It's an adventure, and every day is different. Our summer sojourns have enabled us to live in the shadow of Mt. Rushmore, to be captivated by the sand and surf of North Carolina's Outer Banks, to experience mile-high living in Colorado, and, at this writing, to be thrilled by the Lakes area of Maine. The scenery is stunning.

"We visit areas of the country we have not seen but would like to explore and look for campgrounds where we [can] find employment," Jane noted. "Usually, we work about 20 hours each week in exchange for our site, which includes water, sewer, and electricity. If we work additional hours, we are paid a modest salary, which helps with the price of fuel. Because the jobs are seasonal and part-time, we have been fortunate to have had many offers and opportunities. In fact, many campground managers have told us how much they enjoy having seniors on their staff. RVing and working at campsites have been great experiences and are fun ways to meet interesting people from all walks of life. We are loving it," Jane said.

REASON 3: YOUR JOB IS CHANGING

My friend Larry, who is a scientist, retired from the federal government after 35 years. He was 60 when he decided to leave. He told me that he had been undecided about retiring that early, but that organizationally, his agency was in a state of flux that he felt was not personally satisfying.

A year before he left, Larry said, potential budget cutbacks had caused major personnel reassignments in the agency, and he had been moved to a position that was far afield from his specialty. In addition, old-timers were being offered buyouts to encourage them to leave.

So he assessed his situation and tried to figure out whether he could afford to retire. He decided he could. His government pension would be about 45 percent of his salary, and in two years he would be eligible for a small monthly Social Security benefit because he had taught college classes part-time for many years. He also would continue to earn money from teaching, and he planned to accept a three-year research fellowship that paid fairly well. "The money and research combined made it interesting," he said of the fellowship. At that point, Larry said, it seemed like a good time to leave. And he did.

"It was time for me to be unhooked from an unchallenging position and to get more involved in what really interested me, which was teaching and scientific study," Larry said.

Three Good Reasons for Not Retiring

REASON 1: WORK IS YOUR IDENTITY

It sounds contradictory: you can be ready to retire but not ready to give up work. What does that mean? It means that work is a habit that is hard to break. As strange as it may seem, especially on those dreadful days when everything is going wrong, work is an integral and even a necessary part of our lives.

Many of us began working as teenagers and have never really stopped. In our early years, our jobs provided the money that made it possible for us to pay for the necessities of life. Later on, our work made it possible for us to pay for some of the luxuries of life. But for most of us, the meaning of work goes far beyond our paychecks. Our jobs and careers have given us our greatest challenges and our highest achievements. They have helped us find our roles in society. And, for better or worse, our work has become our identity.

Soon after I retired, I began having identity problems. For 23 years, I had been calling people on the telephone and saying, "This is Stan Hinden of the *Washington Post*." After I left the newspaper, when I made a phone call, I was just "Stan Hinden," and I felt that I had lost a piece of my identity.

This problem sometimes cropped up at social gatherings when I was meeting people for the first time. At these affairs, people looking for conversational openings often ask each other, "What kind of work do you do?" In American life, it is common for people to measure the worth and value of other people by their work and their titles. This tendency is unfortunate, but it happens all the time.

After I retired and people asked me what kind of work I did, I tended to stumble. I found myself saying, "Well, I'm retired. But I used to be a writer at the *Washington Post*." The phrase "used to be" didn't come easily to my lips. It was like saying, "I'm a has-been." And I didn't like that feeling one bit.

Thus, I found that not only did retirement tamper with my identity and my image of myself, but it put me in a "has-been" category that was uncomfortable for someone who had led a vigorous working life.

REASON 2: YOU'LL MISS THE PEOPLE YOU WORK WITH

The idea of not having to go to your job every day may seem mighty attractive, but ask yourself this question: "Am I really ready to give up working and everything that goes with it?" That "everything" includes not only the challenges and frustrations of your job, but also the familiar, even welcome, daily routines at work.

Ask yourself also, "Will I miss the people I work with?"

These are not facetious questions. Although we like to scoff at the idea that we love our jobs, work plays an important role in our lives. It provides us with a sense of purpose and accomplishment and, of course, a place to go in the morning. For many of us, our workplace is our home away from home, the place where we spend time with a network of friends and colleagues.

That network tends to dissolve quickly when you retire and step out of the working world, as I found when I retired from the *Post* after a 45-year career as a reporter, editor, and columnist. So it's not surprising to me that many retirees say that they miss work—or at least, they miss the friends and shared experiences that they had at work.

This sense of loss hit me after I retired from my job as a financial writer at the *Post* and before I went back to writing part-time. It took me quite a while to figure out why, even though I loved retirement, I seemed to miss working. I was puzzled.

I knew, of course, why I liked retirement: it gave me that wonderful sense of freedom that I mentioned earlier. After 45 years of working, it was delightful to be able to live by my own timetable. But why, then, did I miss working? Eventually, it dawned on me that what I really missed was not my work, but my *workplace*.

My office had been my second home, a place where I could chat with friends, catch up on gossip, swap office rumors, and help the other Monday morning quarterbacks decide what to do with the Washington Redskins. When I left the paper, I left all that behind. And I missed it.

REASON 3: YOU WANT TO STAY IN THE LOOP

My friend Bert Ely is 70 years old, an age at which most people either have retired or are thinking about it. But Bert is not headed in that direction. A prominent Washington consultant in the field of banking and financial services, Bert has run his own business for 40 years. And he plans to continue to do just that.

A man of high energy, Bert says he does not ever want to retire. "While eventually I might like to trim my present 60-hour workweek to 50 hours or even 40 hours and take a few longer weekends," he told me, "continuing to work full-time still seems much more attractive, invigorating, and fun than the alternatives." At the same time, he has found striking a good balance between his professional and his civic activities to be a challenge. "When you don't charge for your services, it is easy to give away too much time, to the detriment of one's professional activities," he said.

Bert says he is aware that if he wants to avoid retirement, especially as he ages, he will face certain professional challenges. He focuses on those challenges by asking himself some hard questions: "How do I stay relevant in my field? What is the best way to maintain professional contacts and to interact positively with much younger peers while maintaining their respect? How do I avoid coming across as an old fogy who is trying to hang on when he should hang it up?"

A top priority, he says, is staying in touch with the people and the issues in his industry. "I'm a great believer in schmoozing, staying in the loop, knowing who the players are, being current on the gossip," he says. Staying up to date technologically is important, too. "My BlackBerry is always close at hand."

Staying relevant, Bert adds, has little to do with age and a lot to do with "not thinking old." "I suspect," he says, "that there are people out there at the age of 85 who are more relevant, more in the loop about what's going on, than some people age 50."

Retiring and Working: Having It Both Ways

The line between work and retirement is becoming more blurred all the time. The fact is that many people who retire go back to work part-time, and some even go back full-time. People are living longer and want to remain involved and productive.

Several of my retired friends have gone back to work part-time or full-time.

Bill Backer retired after 38 years at General Electric and then went back to work at GE under the company's Golden Opportunity program, which allowed retirees to work up to 1,000 hours a year. A marketing specialist, Bill worked about 1,000 hours a year, helping GE organize trade shows and exhibits.

Now 86, Bill worked part-time for 14 years and was enthusiastic about his "retirement" job. One main reason: "I had long-standing friendships where I had worked." These days, he said, he continues to see those friends and former GE colleagues at regular retiree luncheons.

A few years ago, Bill and his wife, Lori, sold the house in which they had lived for 42 years and moved to a nearby retirement community. The community offers a full schedule of social and intellectual activities—more than enough, Bill said, to keep him and his wife busy.

My friend Jerry Goldberg, who is 85, completed a 30-year career in the dry-cleaning business. He then worked full-time for 15½ years as a school-bus driver and bus attendant in Montgomery County, Maryland.

Several years ago, Jerry suffered a mini-stroke and had to give up driving. After that, he helped handicapped children get on and off the bus and rode along with them. Jerry says he liked the health and vacation benefits that came with his job and his pay.

Eventually, Jerry said, he felt it was time to give up his school-bus job and retire. But because he was energetic, he started working as a volunteer at Montgomery General Hospital in Olney, Maryland. He now spends four hours a week helping the staff in the emergency room at the hospital.

Jerry's experience is a reminder that there is another factor that is left out of all the hype about people happily working in retirement—one's health. Our ability to work depends on the state of our health. Try as we might, good health is not always in our control.

Until the 2008–2009 market crash and recession severely eroded the retirement savings of millions of Americans, it was thought that there would be an explosion of part-time retired workers when members of the baby-boom generation—77 million people born between 1946 and 1964—started to retire. Indeed, the steady march into retirement began in 2008 when some of the oldest boomers took early Social Security benefits at age 62. But the "explosion" of part-time workers didn't happen quite the way it was predicted.

The retirement/part-time work picture changed dramatically after the market crash in 2008. An AARP study in May 2008 reported that 27 percent of all workers 45 and older had postponed their plans to retire. Among their reasons: losses in 401(k) plans, sharp declines in home values, and rising prices for gasoline and utilities. Note that this survey was taken *before* job losses raised the U.S. unemployment rate to 10 percent. In short, many boomers who had planned to retire suddenly elected to stay on the job—and felt fortunate to have a job in the midst of a deep recession.

Inevitably, when the national economy recovers and people become more comfortable with the decision to retire, there will once again be many retirees working part-time.

Several precrash surveys reported that 80 to 85 percent of boomers planned to continue working—at least part-time—after retirement. While a relatively small number of people said that they expected to work because they needed the money, most said that they wanted to keep busy or pursue individual goals. A significant number of people indicated that they wanted to start their own businesses.

The changing nature of retirement and work was described by Neal Cutler, former director of survey research at the National Council on Aging (NCOA) in Washington, DC. "We will see more and more people who describe themselves as retired but continue to work," Cutler said. "Many of these people are working by choice, not because they have to. In the twenty-first century, retirement will encompass a wide range of options. We will see some 75-year-olds working two jobs and some 40-year-olds lounging poolside.

"Retirement," Cutler continued, "used to be defined by what one was no longer doing—not parenting, not working, not actively involved. Increasingly it will be defined by what one does do— second career, volunteer work, travel, sports activities."

Cutler's comments accompanied the findings of a national survey taken by Harris Interactive, Inc., for the NCOA and the International Longevity Center. The survey showed that most Americans no longer think you've reached old age simply because you've turned 60 or 65 or 70.

Only 14 percent of those surveyed said that reaching a specific age indicated that you were old. By contrast, 41 percent said that a decline in physical ability meant that you were getting old. And 32 percent said that a decline in mental ability was an indicator of old age.

As chronological age becomes less of a factor in retirement thinking, good health becomes more of a factor in keeping retirees active. Among those surveyed who responded that they were retired, 15 percent said that they continued to work full-time, while 35 percent said that they did volunteer work. That means that half of American retirees are not spending their time turning into couch potatoes. Unfortunately, the survey doesn't tell us what the other half are doing.

In my case, eight months after I retired, I went back to work part-time, writing a column on retirement and writing freelance articles. I was fortunate. The column acted as a bridge between my full-time, 100-miles-an-hour working life and what could have been a zero-miles-an-hour retirement. Writing columns for the *Post* helped me ease into retirement gradually.

Better yet, it allowed me to stay in touch with my colleagues at the newspaper. I was happy to go to the office occasionally to pick up mail, chat with old friends, or go to lunch with business contacts. For me, it was the best of both worlds.

Retiring with Your Spouse: The Togetherness Test

When you start to weigh the pros and cons of retiring, take a few minutes to think about what your life will be like after you leave your job—especially if you are married.

When my wife, Sara, and I retired from the business world, one of the questions we faced was, "What will it be like to stay at home and spend 24 hours a day with each other?"

Although we had been married for more than 40 years, we had no idea what the answer would be. In all those years, we had never been home together full-time. After our marriage, Sara spent 18 years at home raising our three children. Then she went to work at GE.

We both held busy, demanding jobs. Sara worked an early shift and I worked a late shift, so we didn't see each other on weekdays for more than a few hours. On weekends, our time was taken up with chores, family activities, or social engagements. In short, there wasn't much time to be bored. If we had a quarrel, we could go to our respective offices the next day and cool off.

Our way of life changed dramatically when Sara retired from GE and I retired from the *Post*. Gone were the established routines of office life and the constant demands of our jobs. We enjoyed a new sense of freedom, but it was accompanied by a feeling that we weren't exactly the same people any longer—that we'd lost our purpose in life.

As the years went by, our concerns about full-time togetherness faded, and we adjusted reasonably well to our new lifestyle. How were we able to do that? There were two main reasons.

First, Sara and I did not go through the "turf battle" that causes problems for many retired couples. A turf battle can arise when a woman who views the home as her domain finds that her retired husband is underfoot all day and interferes with her routine. She may feel that her territory has been invaded. He may feel that he is unwelcome in his own home—and be unable to understand why.

A glimpse of the problem can be seen in the old joke about the wife who says to her newly retired husband, "Just remember, I married you for better or for worse. But not for lunch."

Sara and I avoided a turf battle in part because she had had a long career at GE. So, while she did not escape the daily household chores that fall to most working women, she had not been a full-time homemaker for two decades before her retirement.

In addition, shortly before we retired, we sold our house and moved to an apartment. The effect was to create a new domain where neither of us had any territorial claims.

Second, Sara and I organized our lives so that we had both time alone and time together. Sara retired first. By the time I retired 2½ years later, she'd already developed a schedule of social and community activities that kept her busy on Mondays, Tuesdays, and Wednesdays.

I quickly realized that Sara's schedule was an opportunity for me to get both the "space" and the time that I needed to work on my freelance writing, take care of the family finances, and exercise at the community fitness room.

So, for part of the week, we each had our own schedule. In time, with Sara's help, I began to understand the need that women have for the companionship of other women. Sara explained that her games, lunches, and shopping trips all helped to fill that need.

"I like to spend time with my women friends and talk about the things women are interested in," Sara told me.

Living in a retirement community, I've also observed that retired men don't make new friends with other men as easily as retired women make new friends with other women. Several men have told me that they miss their male colleagues at the office and all the chatter about football, baseball, basketball, and the like.

On Thursdays, Fridays, Saturdays, and Sundays, Sara and I did things together: going to a new Smithsonian museum exhibition in Washington, DC, taking a day trip with friends to the Eastern Shore of Maryland, or just visiting a shopping mall. I preferred museums to malls; Sara preferred malls. We kept the peace by taking turns.

We also solved the weekly food-shopping problem: we did it together. For years, Sara had done almost all the food shopping, often after a long day's work. Once I retired, I didn't think she should continue to lug all those grocery bags herself.

In the beginning, our shopping experiences were quite tense. We had different priorities about what to buy and different recollections of what food items were still in the cupboard or the refrigerator. Apparently we were not alone in this, because we'd frequently hear couples arguing in the aisles about what to buy or not to buy.

We both hated that scene. So I promised myself that when Sara picked an item off the shelf, I would stop saying, "Do we really need that?" After that, our shopping excursions became more relaxed.

On evenings when we ate at home, Sara and I got through dinner by using a team approach: she cooked and I cleaned up.

The system had a double benefit. The meal was always excellent because of Sara's culinary skills, and that made me happy. And Sara didn't have to deal with the mess, which made her happy.

This is the kind of partnership that married people should strive for at all stages of their lives. But it's especially important when they're both retired.

Sara believed that if a couple wants to be happy in retirement, they need to be even more compatible than they were before they retired.

"When you retire, you'd better be friends," Sara said, "because you're going to be spending a lot of time together."

Can I Afford to Retire?

Now that you've decided that you're ready to retire—or at least decided that you're ready to think about it seriously—let's talk about whether you can afford to retire.

On the face of it, the arithmetic of retirement is fairly simple. It's a matter of income versus expenses. The key question is, will your monthly income be sufficient to cover your monthly expenses?

To get started, take a sheet of paper. On one side, list all the elements of monthly income that you expect to receive after you retire. Add them up. On the other side of the paper, list all your monthly expenses and add them up. Then compare the numbers to see whether you have enough income to cover your expenses.

If you do have enough income, you're off to a good start. If you don't, you have two basic choices: you can raise your income, or you can lower your expenses. Either of these, as I learned from personal experience, is easier said than done.

However, there is another choice: you can use your savings to help close the gap between your income and your expenses. Using your savings is a perfectly reasonable idea. After all, that's why you saved the money in the first place. However, you must plan your withdrawals carefully; you don't want to dig into your savings too often or too deeply. Your nest egg may have to help support you for 15 or 20 years. In Decision 7, we'll discuss how you can use your savings to provide a flow of monthly income.

The Change in Your Financial Situation

One of the things that surprised me about retirement was the dramatic way in which my financial situation suddenly changed. One day I was receiving a sizable paycheck. The next day, it seemed, my paychecks had stopped. Intellectually, I was aware that my paychecks would stop when I retired. But I guess I wasn't fully prepared for the emotional jolt of losing that lifelong security blanket.

In fact, there were several other major financial differences between working and retirement that I hadn't anticipated. Here are some of them.

HELLO, FIXED INCOME

As full-time retirees, Sara and I are now living on a fixed income consisting mainly of our monthly Social Security benefits and our pension checks. We are fortunate to have pension checks. These days, many people do not receive pensions when they retire.

But even if you get both Social Security benefits and a pension check, they are not likely to increase much over time. Most pensions are not adjusted for increases in the cost of living. Social Security usually gives its beneficiaries a modest annual cost-of-living adjustment (COLA). However, a COLA is not guaranteed. Because inflation was modest in 2010 and 2011 there were no COLAs. The 2012 COLA was 3.6 percent. The COLA for 2013 is 1.7 percent.

GOOD-BYE, RAISES

When we were employed full-time, our salaries were subject to occasional improvement. We were eligible for raises and promotions, both of which boosted our incomes. We were able to work overtime, which also increased our take-home pay. And, we occasionally received bonuses. In short, there was a reasonable chance that we could increase the amount of money we made each year. As retirees, we don't have those opportunities.

That means that the raises, overtime, and bonuses that helped pay for our new cars and summer vacations when we were working are not available in our retirement years. We have to find other ways to pay for large-ticket purchases or trips.

HEALTHCARE COSTS

Healthcare costs are likely to increase in retirement. In fact, the nonpartisan Employee Benefit Research Institute (EBRI) in Washington recently studied the likely costs of healthcare in retirement. This is what the researchers found.

In 2010, a married couple with median drug expenses would need $158,000 to have a 50 percent chance of having enough money to cover healthcare expenses in retirement and $271,000 to have a 90 percent chance.

Since EBRI's other studies show that relatively few people have this much money in savings when they retire, the question is, "Where will the money come from?" In my case, the money for our insurance premiums and other healthcare costs has come largely from current income. I suspect this is true for many other retirees, as well.

While Sara and I were working, we both had company health insurance that covered our medical, dental, and prescription bills. When we retired, we lost our company insurance.

Fortunately, we were both over 65 and thus were eligible to receive Medicare benefits. However, had we retired at age 62—an age at which many people retire—we could have been without health insurance for several years. The alternative would have been to buy private insurance until we were old enough to go on Medicare. That insurance would have been quite costly—and would have made a rather large hole in our retirement budget.

Neither of our employers had retiree health insurance plans available for us, so we signed up for Medicare, a national program that pays hospital and medical bills for 47 million people. In 2006, Medicare also began to pay for prescription drugs. In fairness to our former employers, the *Washington Post* provides retirees with an annual cash stipend that can be used to buy a secondary insurance policy. General Electric, for its part, provides its retirees with a secondary insurance policy that costs $206 a month for the two of us—a relative bargain. Equally important, GE allows its retirees and their spouses to join a prescription benefit plan that provides a 90-day supply of a medication for $35.

When you begin working on your retirement budget, don't forget that you probably will have to buy a secondary insurance or Medigap policy to cover some of the expenses that Medicare does not pay for. I'll discuss Medigap policies and their cost in Decision 8. You also may have to pay for some of your prescription drugs, as payments under the Medicare Part D prescription drug program are limited.

The bottom line is that Sara and I are spending more money on our healthcare in retirement than we did while we were working and had company coverage—even though we paid for our company coverage.

Medicare, by the way, does not cover all hospital or medical costs. Our GE secondary insurance plan covers some of the bills that Medicare does not pay. Even with that, however, our annual out-of-pocket expenses for healthcare are perhaps 50 percent higher than our expenses when we were working.

We also worried—whether we would encounter new medical problems and thus face even higher costs in the years ahead. Medical costs can be real budget busters.

When you are thinking about how much healthcare money to include in your retirement budget, you may want to consider the cost of a long-term-care policy. For a 62-year-old couple, these policies can cost about $7,980 a year, depending on the terms of the policy. For a 52-year-old couple, the cost would be about $6,128 a year. Sara and I are covered by a group policy that we bought through the *Washington Post*. It costs $2,800 a year for both of us, which is relatively inexpensive, but it has limited benefits. I'll discuss long-term-care policies in Decision 9.

THE TAXMAN COMETH

In your retirement budget, you may need to include a special reserve for the money you owe for federal and state income taxes. During the years I worked, my employer always withheld money from my paycheck for income taxes. Usually, the amount of my withholding would be close to the actual amount of money I owed Uncle Sam at tax time, so it was easy to settle up with the IRS.

When I retired, I neglected to ask the *Post* to put tax withholding on my pension check. My Social Security check also did not have withholding. Sara and I later asked for withholding to be put on our pension checks, but we have not gotten around to putting withholding on our Social Security checks. (To do so, fill out IRS Form W-4V, Voluntary Withholding Request, and submit it to your local Social Security office.)

The effect of not having withholding on our Social Security and pension checks was that I had to file quarterly estimated income tax reports with the IRS and my state tax office. It also meant that I had to put aside a certain amount of money each month to cover the quarterly payments. Initially, I wasn't used to doing that, and it played havoc with my efforts to balance my family budget.

Here is something else you should be aware of when it comes to taxes in retirement: your Social Security payments may be taxable. Ignoring the fact that you paid taxes on the money you put into Social Security for many, many years, Uncle Sam will tax up to 85 percent of your Social Security benefits, depending on your income and your tax situation.

Indeed, it is a good idea to talk to an accountant before you retire to find out what your tax situation will be and what effect those taxes will have on the amount of money you'll have available to pay for your living expenses.

MORE ABOUT THE TAXMAN

As I will explain in Decisions 5 and 6, the beauty of 401(k) and IRA plans is that they permit you to save money in a tax-deferred account for many years while you are working. Such accounts can reward you by producing a sizable retirement nest egg. But when you reach the magic age of 70½ years, Uncle Sam says you have to start withdrawing money from these accounts and paying taxes on your withdrawals.

As you prepare your retirement budget, especially if you are nearing 70½, remember that every dollar you withdraw from a tax-deferred IRA will be taxable. If, for instance, your taxable income is $40,000 and you take a $10,000 IRA withdrawal, your taxable income will become $50,000, and you will be taxed accordingly. So here again, you may need to set aside money in your budget for taxes—money that you'd probably prefer to spend on other things.

Paying for Your Lifestyle

As you prepare to retire, you will hear a great deal of discussion about what percentage of your working income you will need to maintain the same lifestyle in retirement. You will hear financial advisors and others suggest that you will need about 80 percent of your regular income when you retire. That figure seems to assume that your living expenses as a retiree will be lower than they were when you were working full-time. Well, maybe yes and maybe no.

The 80 percent rule didn't work for us. If anything, our living costs in retirement have been higher than they were when we were both working. It makes sense if you think about it this way: when we retired, we did not relocate to a less expensive community, as some of our friends did. We stayed in the apartment that we had moved into a few years before we retired. Our mortgage payments remained about the same, but our condo fees rose. Our food bills went up, too, keeping pace with the general increase in food prices. We have also been eating more restaurant meals than we used to—probably because we were home more and had more free time.

As for clothing, I haven't bought a new suit in some time—I don't need them much for business anymore—but there's been an increase in the amount of casual clothing that Sara and I have bought in recent years.

Moreover, early in our retirement, we continued to drive two cars because Sara and I were always going in different directions and we needed the freedom that having two cars provided. After a few years, as the pace of our activities slowed, we were able to get along with one car. That decision saved us quite a bit of money on auto insurance, gasoline, and repairs.

Yes, we did save some money because we were not commuting to work every day—but not that much. We probably used the same amount of gas visiting our local shopping malls.

Other expenses, such as our electric and telephone bills, have either remained the same or gone up. For instance, Sara and I have cell phones for highway emergencies and for the convenience of being able to stay in touch with family and friends.

Our budget also changed when it came to entertainment. Going out to dinner with friends is the number-one leisure-time activity in our part of the country. We also subscribed to several local theater groups and have attended their shows regularly, something we hadn't had time for when we were working. Tickets for those shows usually cost $60 to $80 each.

Our retirement savings, I confess, took a big hit when we began to travel after we retired. We had both worked for many, many years, and we felt that we were entitled to enjoy some of the pleasures that go with retirement. So we took several cruises. Our cruise to Scandinavia and Russia was memorable, but the cost of our trip was about $15,000, in part because it included a week of sightseeing in London.

My point is that when you are planning your retirement, it is foolhardy to think that you will be happy living like a pauper. You don't live that way now while you are working, and there's no reason you should plan to live that way when you retire.

At the very least, make sure that your income and your expenses—adjusted for the factors I have mentioned—allow you to have the kind of lifestyle to which you have become accustomed. Remember, too, that you will want to have some fun in retirement. But the cost of that fun will be extra.

If your arithmetic shows that you can maintain your lifestyle and also have some fun, then you can afford to retire. But if your retirement numbers show that you can't make ends meet, even with judicious withdrawals from savings, then you may have to delay your retirement and keep working until your finances improve.

For instance, continuing to work past your full retirement age, now 66 for many people, can improve your retirement income in two ways. First, Social Security provides a bonus for every year you work past the normal retirement age up to age 70. The normal age for retirement has been moving up gradually from 65 to 66 and will rise to 67 in the future. If you are 66 in 2013 and you wait until age 70 to take your Social Security benefits, you will receive four years of delayed retirement credit and a bonus of 32 percent. Thus a $1,000 monthly Social Security payment will turn into about $1,320.

Second, if you are entitled to a pension from your company and you continue to work, your pension may improve because of your additional earnings and because of pay raises. If your retirement budget looks as if it could be tight, find out how much money you will receive both from Social Security and from your company pension if you work until age 70—assuming that your company will let you work until that age.

I retired at the age of 69 and found that both my Social Security and my pension were considerably higher than they would have been if I had retired at 65. Waiting to retire turned out to be a big help financially.

THE POWER OF TIME

When I step back and look at the list of items I have just dis-cussed—the items that can seriously affect one's retirement bud-get—it is hard for me not to wish that I had saved more money during my working years. Indeed, I often wish that I had been wiser or more farsighted in building my retirement nest egg.

I'm not complaining. We did not save as much as some of our friends, but we saved more than others, so we're somewhere in the middle. And while we're reasonably secure financially, we still have to worry about whether we could run out of money during our retirement.

Perhaps if we had started saving earlier, we wouldn't have to worry about that. In recent years, I've learned that what you do about your money when you are 30, 40, or 50 will determine whether you can retire comfortably at 60, 65, or 70.

Ideally, wise or foresighted individuals will begin to save regu-larly at age 30, putting aside as much money as he or she can, month after month and year after year, for 30 or 35 years. Then, if the financial markets do what they have done for the last 75 or 83 years, the savers should reach retirement age with a sizable pot of money—enough to pay for a comfortable retirement, even if it lasts for 20 or 25 years. Admittedly, that optimistic scenario took quite a jolt during the 2008–2009 market crash. Millions of investors suffered 30 to 40 percent losses, or more, in their mutual fund accounts. People who were close to retirement were especially badly hurt. Indeed, as mentioned, many individuals postponed their retirements. People who were already retired could only look at their paper losses and hope that they had enough time to wait for the market to "come back."

In my younger years, trying to save money was a frustrating experience. As a young reporter, I was married and had three children, a small house, a big mortgage, and a salary on which I could barely make ends meet. My wife was a stay-at-home mom, so we had to manage on my modest newspaper salary. Saving money was a near impossibility.

In the 1950s, the 401(k) plan had not yet been invented, and U.S. savings bonds were the most common vehicles for saving money, except perhaps for the annual Christmas Club at the local bank. In any event, I was like most young people. For me, retirement was a word that had little meaning. When I turned 40 in 1967, people were "old" at 65 and were thought to be lucky if they reached the biblical goal of "three score and ten," or 70.

The concept of a long, healthy retirement that took people into their eighties or nineties had not yet emerged. It was not until the 1980s, and especially the 1990s, that saving for retirement became a national mantra, aided by the aging of the nation's 77 million baby boomers, the growth of the 401(k) plan, and the hype of the mutual fund industry.

Looking back to when I was 40, I can see why it's so hard to talk to people in their thirties and forties about retirement and to convince them to save for the future. The first problem, of course, is that when you're that age, retirement seems just too far away to worry about. The second problem is that when you're that age, there's a good chance that your monthly bills are eating up every penny you bring home.

Basically, that's what happened to me. It wasn't until I was 50 or 55 years old, after my children were grown and out on their own, after my salary had improved, and after my wife had returned to work, that we got a chance to do some serious saving.

While that was the good news, the bad news was that we had wasted many years that could have helped us achieve our retirement savings goals. And that was a shame, because in the battle for financial survival, the best weapon is time itself. I believe sincerely that when it comes to building your nest egg, it is almost as great a sin to waste time as it is to waste money.

Time can turn a modest amount of regular savings into a hefty amount of money. If you invest $100 a month for 15 years at a rate of 6 percent, you will wind up with $29,082. On the other hand, if you invest $100 a month at the same interest rate for 30 years, you will wind up with $100,452, more than three times as much.

The number of dollars you put into an investment is important, of course. But this example shows that the amount of time you give an investment is equally important. Why? Because money makes money.

People in the financial community often tell a story that may or may not be factual, but that makes an important point about saving. The story is that Albert Einstein, the eminent physicist, was once asked, "Professor, in your opinion, what is the greatest invention the world has ever known?" Einstein thought for a moment and then replied, "Compound interest!"

Now, compound interest sounds like a mysterious concept if you're not familiar with it. But it's not. Here's a simple example. Let's say you invest $100 at 6 percent interest a year and never add to it. In the first year, the $100 earns $6 in interest. You then have $106. In the second year, the $106 earns 6 percent, or $6.36, giving you a total of $112.36. In the third year, the account grows to $119.10, and so on. If you let your $100 grow and compound over 20 years, you will wind up with $321. In other words, your money will more than triple in 20 years, even though you never added another dollar to your account.

The power of compound interest can be quite awesome, especially when it is given enough time.

How to Make Your Money Grow

Now that we can see how money grows, the next question is, "What's the best way to make your money grow in those all-important years before retirement?" There are, to be sure, many choices. But some of them are particularly worthwhile, because they come equipped with tax breaks that Uncle Sam hopes will encourage you to save for retirement.

SAVING AT WORK

The most important savings program, in my view, is the 401(k) plan, which many companies offer to their employees. There is a fuller description of 401(k) plans in Decision 5, but here's a brief description of this type of plan and why you should join one if it is available where you work.

Typically, the plan allows you to contribute a percentage of your salary each week or month to a savings account set up in your name. Let's say you put in 6 percent of your pay. Your employer may then match part of your contribution by putting in, say, 3 percent of your pay, for a total contribution of 9 percent.

The company's contribution is often called "free money," but the best part of getting a "company match" is that it increases the number of dollars you have working—and compounding—for you in your account. Professor Einstein would approve.

Many companies hire mutual fund firms to manage the money that goes into their 401(k) plans. In those cases, you and your fellow employees will be given a list of the mutual funds that are available to you. It will then be your responsibility to decide which fund or funds you want to invest your money in.

When it comes to saving, the 401(k) plan has some special advantages. One main advantage is that the money you contribute is deducted from your pay before federal income taxes are withheld. That reduces your income taxes—a welcome, if temporary, tax break. Eventually, you will have to make up for those unpaid taxes—but not until you start to take money out of your account, and that could be many years in the future. Indeed, you could wait until you are age 70½.

The other advantage to tax deferral is that it helps increase the number of dollars in your account that are available to multiply and grow.

The downside of the 401(k) plan is that eventually you have to pay taxes on your withdrawals. Most people feel that this is a small price to pay for the privilege of being able to build a solid nest egg over a period of many years.

One question that I am frequently asked is, "We have a 401(k) plan at work, but my employer doesn't match any of my savings. Should I join the plan and contribute anyway?" I always say yes. It would be better to have the matching money, of course, but you still get a tax break when you put your money into the account, and it still can grow on a tax-deferred basis.

THE ROTH IRA

If you are putting as much money as you are allowed to into your 401(k) plan at work and you have additional money available for investment, you might want to think about opening a Roth IRA. The Roth IRA was named for the late Senator William V. Roth of Delaware, who was chairman of the Senate Finance Committee. Unlike traditional IRAs, which give you a tax deduction when you open them, the Roth IRA does not. If you fall within certain income limits, you can invest up to $5,000 a year in a Roth IRA in 2013. If you are 50 years old or older, you are allowed to invest an additional $1,000 each year.

To be eligible to contribute the maximum amount to a Roth IRA in 2013, a single person must have a modified adjusted gross income of below $110,000 a year. Married couples that file jointly must have an income of below $173,000.

The beauty of a Roth IRA is that after you reach age 59½, if you have owned a Roth IRA for five years, you can take out the earnings, as well as your original contributions, without paying any taxes. Before the five years are up, you can always withdraw some or all of your principal (that is, your after-tax contributions) tax-free if you need it, since with a Roth IRA, principal is deemed to be withdrawn first. Or, if you wish, you can keep the money invested without ever taking it out, leaving it for your heirs—a major benefit when you consider tax-free growth over a long time period. Finally, Roth IRAs are not subject to required minimum distributions (RMDs), which in traditional IRAs often force retirees to take out more than they want to, need to, or have planned to. Those three features can be a major advantage to a retiree.

The Roth IRA came along after I retired, so I did not have a chance to make use of it. But if it had been available when I was younger, I would have tried to fund one each year. Having Roth IRA money available would have been a major advantage after I retired.

While Sara and I are grateful for the money we saved in our 401(k) plans at work, every dollar we take out of those accounts is fully taxable. When I reached 70½, I had to start withdrawing money from those accounts, as I explain in Decision 6.

The Roth IRA doesn't give you a tax break when you open or contribute to the account. But it does allow your money to grow tax-deferred over many years. And since you can take it out tax-free, that's a pretty good deal.

CONVERTING AN IRA TO A ROTH IRA

If you have been thinking about converting some or all of your traditional IRA to a Roth IRA, 2013 may be a good year to do so, since there are no income limits on who can do a conversion.

However, you will have to pay income taxes on the amount of money you convert from your traditional IRA to your Roth IRA.

THE ROTH 401(K)

The relatively new Roth 401(k) is similar to a regular 401(k) plan with one main difference: contributions to a Roth 401(k) account are made with after-tax dollars. Thus, when you withdraw money from a Roth 401(k), those dollars are not taxable, provided you meet a special five-year rule and you are at least 59½ years old. In 2013, the maximum you can contribute after tax to a Roth 401(k) at work is $17,500 ($23,000 if you are age 50 or older). However, not all employers offer this new savings vehicle. It's important to note that any matching contributions you receive from your employer will typically be made on a tax-deferred basis, as with a traditional 401(k), instead of on an after-tax basis.

TAX-EFFICIENT FUNDS

If, after fully funding your 401(k) plan at work and contributing to a Roth IRA each year, you still have additional money available, you might consider investing in a "tax-efficient" mutual fund. These funds are aimed at reducing the amount of taxes that shareholders pay each year on distributions. The way they do this is by lowering or eliminating both the dividend income and the capital gains that they would otherwise pass on to shareholders. These twin goals are achieved in several ways. First, tax-efficient funds reduce the amount of buying and selling in their portfolios, thereby minimizing capital gains. Second, they try to avoid capital gains taxes by offsetting gains with losses. Finally, they often invest in low- or no-dividend stocks that are likely to grow in market value but that do not produce income.

Tax-efficient funds are of relatively recent vintage, but they are widely available, especially from major fund companies. Index funds, which have been around for a long time, are also considered tax-efficient because there is relatively little turnover in their portfolios.

Tax-efficient funds are likely to grow in popularity in the coming years, especially if federal and state taxes are raised to make up for the revenue lost during the 2008–2009 recession. As boomers move into higher tax brackets, they will be looking for ways to invest and reduce their taxes.

A Comfortable Retirement

A few years ago, I saw a sign in a Pennsylvania restaurant that said, "Too old, too soon. Too wise, too late." I have never forgotten that bit of wisdom because it seemed to summarize my regrets about not paying closer attention to my personal finances when I was younger. It now seems perfectly obvious that I should have saved more aggressively during my working years. Social Security and pensions are helpful, but it is our savings that will make it possible for us to have a comfortable retirement. So save as much as you can. And when you finally sit down to draw up your retirement budget, your income will outweigh your expenses, and you'll be able to say, "Yes, I can afford to retire."

For More Information

BOOKS

Slesnick, Twila, and John C. Suttle. *IRAs, 401(k)s and Other Retirement Plans—Taking Your Money Out*. Berkeley, CA: Nolo, 2009.

Slott, Ed. *Your Complete Retirement Planning Road Map*. New York: Ballantine Books, 2008.

Thomas, Kaye A. *Go Roth: Your Guide to the Roth IRA, Roth 401(k) and Roth 403(b)*. Elgin, IL: Fairmark Press Inc., 2012.

WEBSITES

Todorova, Aleksandra. "Understanding the Roth 401(k)." Smart Money. http://www.smartmoney.com/personal-finance/retirement/understanding-the-roth-401k-17679/.

When Should I Apply for Social Security?

Life is full of milestones. There are graduations and weddings, birthdays and anniversaries, and many other memorable events. Retirement is one of those milestones. I remember the day I picked up the telephone, dialed 1-800-772-1213, and told a representative of the Social Security Administration (SSA) that I was ready to apply for retirement benefits.

Several years have passed since I made that phone call, but I can clearly recall that I was nervous as I notified the U.S. government that at the age of 69, I had decided to retire. I guess I was nervous because making that call was akin to saying to myself, "OK, pal, this is it. Your retirement is official. There's no going back."

After that, it took me a while to realize how quickly that phone call to the SSA changed my status in life. One moment I was an active, hardworking member of the American workforce with a paycheck coming in regularly. The next moment, I was a retired person who would henceforth depend on Social Security benefits to help me pay for my living expenses.

I wasn't entirely comfortable with the idea of being so dependent on Social Security. But it was exhilarating to think that after 50 years of contributing to the system, I was finally going to get something back. At that point, I wasn't sure how much I would get each month, but I knew that it would be an important part of my retirement income. I was also comforted by knowing that the payments would continue for the rest of my life.

In fact, it was only after Sara and I had decided to retire— and applied for our benefits—that we began to learn how Social Security works. Fortunately, we had not needed any of the agency's support services earlier in our lives. But that meant that we'd had no occasion to learn about the workings of its many benefit programs.

I realize now that I arrived at retirement age with little knowledge of the role that Social Security plays in our national life. Nor did I understand the value of the safety net that the SSA provides for millions of elderly and disabled Americans and for families that have lost their breadwinners.

Like many Americans, I tended to think of Social Security as a savings bank. I thought that the payroll taxes taken out of my salary each payday would be deposited in Washington, earn interest, and eventually be returned to me when I retired. I could not have been more wrong, for that is not the way the system works.

Social Security, I discovered, is not a bank at all. It is, essentially, a national social insurance program that uses the taxes paid by American workers and their employers to create a giant pool of money. It's a pay-as-you-go system, in the sense that the money that goes into the pool is then paid out to people who are eligible for benefits. Indeed, one of the main concerns about the future of Social Security is that a time will come when there will be far fewer people putting money into the pool relative to the number taking money out.

The key goal of Social Security is to provide a minimum income—sometimes called a "floor of protection"—for workers and their families. Among these individuals are people who reach retirement age, workers who become disabled, and families that lose their wage earners. An estimated 94 percent of all American workers contribute to the system.

Social Security's programs provide valuable income protection to disabled persons and surviving family members. Here are some examples. For a person earning a medium wage with a spouse age 28 and two children (a two-year-old and a newborn) who became disabled at age 30 in 2008, the "insurance value" of disability benefits up to age 67 was equal to a $329,000 disability policy. In addition, if this worker had died at age 30, the income protection to the survivors would have been equal to a $476,000 life-insurance policy.

Clearly, Social Security is more than a retirement program, and the SSA's figures show that to be true. In 2011, almost 55 million Americans received almost $725 billion in benefits. Here's how the $725 billion were shared:

- Sixty-four percent of the benefits went to nearly 38.4 million retired workers and their dependents. The average monthly benefit was $1,182.

- Fifteen percent went to more than 10.6 million disabled workers and their dependents. The average monthly benefit was $960.

- Eight percent went to nearly 6.3 million survivors of deceased workers. The average monthly payment was $1,036.

The importance of the safety net becomes even more apparent when you dig into those figures and find that:

- Social Security benefits were received by 88 percent of married couples and 86 percent of nonmarried persons aged 65 and older.

- Social Security was the major source of income (providing at least 50 percent of total income) for 53 percent of aged beneficiary couples and 73 percent of aged nonmarried beneficiaries.

- Social Security provided 90 percent or more of the income of 22 percent of aged beneficiary couples and 43 percent of aged nonmarried beneficiaries.

What Are Your Benefits Based On?

When it comes time to pay benefits to retirees, how does the agency decide who gets what? It's a question I had never thought about, and I doubt whether many other people have done so either. The fact is that there is a specific social philosophy that determines the payment of benefits, and this philosophy has several components. For instance, the formulas are designed so that there is a clear link between what you pay into the system during your working years and the benefits you receive when you retire. People who earn high wages during their careers generally will get higher benefits than people who earn low wages.

However, one key feature of the payment philosophy tends to level the playing field: the formula used to compute benefits includes factors that ensure that lower-paid workers get a higher return than highly-paid workers. Social Security's progressive benefit structure helps to compensate for the fact that those who earn low wages have less opportunity to save and invest.

Low-wage earners who retired at 66 in January 2013 have about 57.8 percent of their preretirement income replaced by Social Security; high-wage earners have about 35.5 percent of their preretirement income replaced by Social Security.

This idea of paying out benefits based on the relative needs of individuals and their families also applies when the agency deals with the disabled and with families that experience the death of their primary wage earner. For instance, a disabled worker with a family to support will draw higher benefits than a disabled worker with no dependent family.

Inevitably, some people get far less in Social Security benefits than they contributed. Others get far more. A worker who contributes to Social Security for 30 years but dies before she can retire gets no retirement benefit. On the other hand, a widow with two young children whose husband dies at age 35 will draw benefits for many years even though her husband contributed relatively little money to the system.

Looking back, I wish I had learned more about Social Security long before I retired. The agency offers future retirees several retirement options that I did not know about, each with its own advantages and disadvantages. In the end, I might have retired exactly when I did, but it would have been wise for me to learn about my options in advance.

As I said earlier, I retired at the age of 69. I draw a Social Security benefit of $2,202 a month thanks to a lifetime of steady work, salary increases, a blind love of the newspaper business that kept me working for four years past my normal retirement age of 65, and Social Security's cost-of-living adjustments.

Sara, who worked for GE for 22 years, draws a Social Security benefit of $1,404. We're grateful for both payments, as they are an important part of our retirement income.

But as we discovered—somewhat too late, perhaps—the time to start thinking about Social Security is when you are in your fifties or early sixties.

Your first opportunity to retire and receive Social Security benefits comes at age 62. After that, you can start taking benefits at any age, although most people do so by the time they are 70. The choice is yours. But there are several things you should know, because they may affect the timing of your decision.

However, before we discuss retirement options, let's take a small detour to discuss several major changes that are taking place in Social Security's retirement benefits.

RAISING THE RETIREMENT AGE

For as long as anyone can remember, age 65 was the "normal" retirement age. The SSA called age 65 the "full retirement age," meaning that at age 65 you became eligible to receive full retirement benefits.

But that rule began to change when Congress decided to raise the full retirement age from 65 to 67. The change was part of a sweeping 1983 measure that strengthened Social Security's finances.

The 1983 package not only boosted the retirement age, but also boosted payroll tax rates for workers, employers, and the self-employed; delayed cost-of-living adjustments; and levied taxes on benefits received by some high-income beneficiaries. The SSA estimates that between 2009 and 2014 alone, the increase in the retirement age will save the federal government billions of dollars.

Table 3.1 shows the age one must reach to qualify for full Social Security benefits. The upward move from age 65 to age 67, as shown in the table, began in 2003 and affected persons born in 1938. In 2003, an individual born in 1938 who wanted to retire had to be age 65 and 2 months in order to qualify for full retirement benefits. After that, the age for receiving full benefits continued to climb gradually, reaching age 66 in 2009 and rising to age 67 over the 22-year period between 2002 and 2027.

TABLE 3.1 Full Retirement Age Goes from 65 to 66 . . . to 67

YEAR OF BIRTH	FULL RETIREMENT AGE
1937 or earlier	65
1938	65 and 2 months
1939	65 and 4 months
1940	65 and 6 months
1941	65 and 8 months
1942	65 and 10 months
1943–1954	66
1955	66 and 2 months
1956	66 and 4 months
1957	66 and 6 months
1958	66 and 8 months
1959	66 and 10 months
1960 and later	67

Note: Persons will still be able to take their retirement benefits at age 62, but the payments will be reduced.

Source: Social Security Administration.

However, for 11 of those interim years, between 2009 and 2020, the retirement age will remain at 66. It will then resume its upward path, reaching 67 in 2027.

In deciding to increase the retirement age, Congress cited improvements in the health of older people and dramatic increases in life expectancy. Today, at age 65, men can expect to live until almost 82. At age 65, women can look forward to living until 84.

Although 2003 was the first year in which people had to be somewhat older than 65 to retire with full benefits, the impact of the age change was felt for the first time in 2000 by people who retired at age 62.

The following describes how they were affected and how the early-retirement option was changed.

YOUR RETIREMENT OPTIONS

Option 1: Early Retirement

Even though the retirement age is rising to 67, you will still be able to retire at age 62 if you are willing to take a permanently reduced Social Security payment. The idea behind the reduction is this: because you are likely to be receiving benefits for a longer period of time, you get less money per month when you retire at age 62 than you would if you retired at your normal retirement age.

How much is the reduction? Until 2000, if you retired at 62, you got 80 percent of your benefits, a reduction of 20 percent. However, as the retirement age rises from 65 to 67, the deduction for early retirement at 62 will increase gradually to 30 percent. For instance, if your full retirement age was 65 and 2 months and you retired at 62 in 2000, you got only 79.17 percent of your benefits, a reduction of 20.83 percent. If your full retirement age was 65 and 4 months and you retired at 62 in 2001, you got 78.33 percent of your full benefits, a reduction of 21.67 percent. The reduction will increase slowly until it reaches 30 percent for people who retire at age 62 in 2022.

Here's a retirement warning: if you are a married man who is thinking about retiring at 62, you may want to consider the impact that early retirement could have on your spouse. Here is an example.

John Q. Worker retires at 62 and takes a reduced Social Security payment of $750 a month. That figure represents a 25 percent reduction from the $1,000 a month he would have gotten if he had retired at 66. His spouse, Mary Q. Worker, also retires at 62 and gets a benefit of $600 a month.

When John is 70, he dies. Mary is entitled to receive her husband's $750 monthly payment instead of her $600 payment because his is more than hers.

However, while Mary will get $750, it is far less than the $1,350 they were receiving together. If John had waited until he was 66 to retire, he would have gotten $1,000 a month. On his death, Mary also would get $1,000 a month.

Because women tend to outlive men, that's a scenario that is worth thinking about before you make your decision about when to retire.

Option 2: Normal Retirement
You can retire at whatever age you become eligible for full retirement benefits.

One key question you need to consider before taking your benefits when you reach your full retirement age is, "Do you want to delay retirement to increase your monthly Social Security benefit?" To answer this question, consider how the Social Security system works. Your retirement benefits are based on your earnings history and other factors. This means that you will get a specific amount of Social Security benefits over your lifetime if you live to an average age.

If you begin taking benefits early at 62, you will get more monthly payments, but with fewer dollars in each check. If you don't take your benefits until you are at your normal retirement age, you will get fewer monthly checks but with more dollars in each check. In addition, those who work beyond 65 may get additional benefits because of their extra years of work.

Option 3: Late Retirement
You can work past your full retirement, which increases your monthly benefits. For people who turned 66 in 2012, a special yearly credit of 8 percent will be added for each year they delay retirement. The bonus ends at age 70.

People who were born in either 1935 or 1936 and worked until age 70 would get an annual 6 percent bonus for five years,

TABLE 3.2   Social Security Delayed Retirement Credits

YEAR OF BIRTH	YEARLY RATE OF INCREASE (%)
1930	4.5
1931–1932	5.0
1933–1934	5.5
1935–1936	6.0
1937–1938	6.5
1939–1940	7.0
1941–1942	7.5
1943 or later	8.0

Source: Social Security Administration.

or a total of 30 percent more than they would have gotten if they had retired at 65. That bonus rose 0.5 percent every two years after that, reaching 8 percent for people born in 1943 and later.

The increases for delayed retirement are shown in Table 3.2. If you delay your retirement beyond your full retirement age, your Social Security benefits will be increased by a certain percentage, depending on your date of birth. The increase in benefits stops when you reach age 70, even if you continue to delay taking benefits.

In 2027, when the full retirement age will be 67, people who work until age 70 will get only three years of bonus payments.

Which Option Is Best?

After I retired, I began to wonder what is the best age at which to take your retirement benefits. Is it 62, 66, or 70?

The answer is that there is no one "best age" for everyone—even though almost half the people who apply for retirement benefits do so at age 62. There are many reasons why it might be prudent to wait until you are 66 or even 70.

Even so, the decision is a highly personal one, and before you apply for benefits, you should consider these factors: your current cash needs, your health and family longevity, your other sources of retirement income, your future financial needs and obligations, and whether you plan to work in retirement.

It is important to realize that if you live to the average life expectancy for someone your age, you will receive about the same amount in lifetime benefits no matter what age you choose to start receiving benefits. Thus, the question is not how to earn the most total dollars from Social Security but how to choose the size and timing of your monthly benefit.

For example, if you start taking benefits at 62, you will get a reduced payment, but for a longer period of time; if you start at 66, you will get a larger payment, but for a shorter period of time; if you start at 70, you will get the largest check for the shortest time period.

I asked SSA's actuaries to give me an example of how these monthly amounts would differ. They provided a hypothetical example of an individual who retired at 62 in 2012 with career-average indexed earnings of $41,655. If the person took his benefits at 62, he would receive about $1,166 a month. If the same person waited to take benefits until age 66, the monthly payment would be $1,555. If the person waited longer still and took benefits at 70, the payment would be $2,053 a month. Clearly, if you will need the largest payment possible when you reach 70, it might pay to wait.

The folks at SSA are quick to point out that benefit amounts for real individuals could differ significantly from these estimates, depending on the worker's actual earnings and the actual cost-of-living adjustments. Also, since SSA bases your benefit, in part, on your average earnings over a 35-year period, your monthly payment could go up if your peak earning years were to occur between ages 66 and 70. In any event, the total amount of benefits you receive will depend on how long you live.

SOCIAL SECURITY STRATEGIES

In the last few years, researchers have begun studying ways for retirees to maximize the benefits available to them from Social Security. Their studies have focused on a little-used Social Security regulation known as "file and suspend." This provision can give retirees added flexibility when they are trying to decide on the best way to take or delay the Social Security benefits to which they are entitled.

The phrase *file and suspend* means that an individual who has reached full retirement age can file for Social Security benefits and then immediately suspend the payment of those benefits. Why would someone do that? Because it opens the door to several strategies that may prove financially advantageous for a retiree and her spouse. (Although Social Security is gender neutral, I will discuss this question in husband-and-wife terms.)

To help clarify the file and suspend strategy, here is an example of how it works.

Mary Smith, the wife, is 63, and her husband, John Smith, is 62. The full retirement age for both is 66.

Mary applies for Social Security retirement benefits at her full retirement age of 66 and receives $940 a month based on her work record.

One year later, when John turns 66, he applies for his Social Security benefits, which are estimated to be $2,060 a month based on his work record.

Now that John has filed for benefits, Mary is entitled to a spousal benefit. After applying, she will receive a total of $1,030 a month (her own $940 plus an additional $90), making her total benefit one-half the benefit that John receives at his full retirement age.

After John applies for benefits, he voluntarily suspends his benefits. Mary continues to receive $1,030 a month, adjusted each year for the cost-of-living adjustment (COLA).

When John becomes 70 years old, he starts receiving his benefits. Because he waited to collect until age 70, he has earned delayed-retirement credits at the rate of 8 percent a year—or a total increase of 32 percent—plus his COLAs. Let's say that at age 70, John's benefits are about $2,802 a month.

If John dies and Mary survives him, she will be entitled to a widow's benefit of $2,802, which includes John's delayed-retirement credits. By waiting to receive benefits, not only did John earn higher monthly Social Security benefits for himself, but he also will have left Mary with a substantial widow's benefit.

It should be noted that the file and suspend strategy may be useful for some individuals but not for others. Social Security experts point out that the success of the strategy depends heavily on one's longevity. If, in our example, John suspended his benefits at age 66 but died before he reached 70, he would have lost several years of payments.

Prospective retirees should therefore consider the state of their health and whether they come from long-lived families before deciding to suspend their Social Security payments. Also, the strategy may work for individuals who have enough money or investments to support them in retirement until they reach age 70. If they do not, they may not be in a position to suspend their benefits for several years.

According to the SSA, these are the basic rules for file and suspend:

1. A request for voluntary suspension of retirement benefits applies only to the worker, and no adjustment in benefits

will be made to others receiving benefits based on the worker's record, such as a spouse and/or children.

2. Voluntary suspension can be elected during the filing of an initial claim or subsequently to entitlement of benefits in writing or orally. There is no prescribed form or question on the application that is used to elect voluntary suspension. In an initial claim filed in the local Social Security office, the filer will make the request known to the interviewer, and the request will be included in the remarks section of the application. If the claim is filed online, the filer can use the remarks section of the Internet application to request voluntary suspension. Additionally, if suspension is elected subsequent to entitlement, the beneficiary can make the request to Social Security in writing or orally.

3. Once the suspension is elected, it continues until the beneficiary requests resumption of payments or through the month before the attainment of age 70. In either case, payments will resume without a need to file again, with an increase in benefits resulting from the delayed retirement credits.

4. A request for resumption of payments can be either written or oral. It can be made by simply calling the SSA's toll-free number at 1-800-772-1213. The SSA will accept a written letter by mail or an oral or written request if the requestor chooses to visit a local Social Security office.

Who Pays for Social Security Benefits?

We all do. However, because of the recession in 2008–2009, the federal government changed the way in which Americans pay for Social Security and Medicare. To put the matter in context, in the "normal" way we have been paying for Social Security and Medicare, employers and employees pay equal amounts. The tax rate in 2010 was 7.65 percent for employers and the same for employees. Of that amount, 6.2 percent was used to finance Social Security retirement, disability, and survivors' benefits, and 1.45 percent went toward the Medicare program. In 2010, employers withheld 7.65 percent of an employee's wages, up to $106,800. The employer paid a matching amount.

If an employee earned more than $106,800, the employer continued to withhold 1.45 percent of the rest of the worker's wages for Medicare. The employer paid an equal amount.

Self-employed people paid both the employee's and the employer's share of the tax, a total of 15.3 percent. However, self-employed persons could deduct one-half of that amount from their income for tax purposes.

This system was changed by the Tax Relief, Unemployment Insurance Reauthorization, and Job Creation Act of 2010. This act reduced the Social Security payroll tax rate by 2 percent on the portion of the tax paid by the worker in 2011.

The Temporary Payroll Tax Cut Continuation Act of 2011 extended this reduction through the end of February 2012. The Middle Class Tax Relief and Job Creation Act of 2012 further continued it, extending it through December 2012. That meant that for 2011 and 2012, the employer paid 6.2 percent and the employee paid 4.2 percent. The maximum tax base for Social Security was $106,800 in 2010 and 2011. For 2012, it was $110,100. For 2013, it will be $113,700.

As shown in Table 3.3, the amount of wages that can be taxed for Social Security contributions will continue to rise above the $106,800 level each year. By 2016, the maximum wages for Social Security levies are projected to be $128,400.

TABLE 3.3 How Much of Your Income
Will Be Taxed for Social Security?

YEAR	UP TO
2006	$94,200
2007	$97,500
2008	$102,000
2009-2011	$106,800
2012	$110,100
2013	$113,700
2014	$117,900
2015	$123,000
2016	$128,400

Source: Social Security Administration projections.

How Do You Qualify for Social Security?

If you were born in 1929 or later, you will need 40 credits to be eligible for retirement benefits. You earn your credits during your working years. Generally speaking, 40 credits represent 10 years of employment. Here's how eligibility is determined.

During your years of employment, your wages are posted on your Social Security record, and you earn credits based on those wages. The credits are used to determine your eligibility for retirement benefits or for disability or survivor benefits if you should become disabled or die.

In 2013, you receive one credit for each $1,160 of earnings, up to a maximum of four credits per year. The SSA folks predict that, in the future, it will take more dollars to earn a credit than it does today because of the steady national increase in average annual wages.

Note that when it comes to qualifying for retirement benefits, there are special rules for the self-employed, for people in the military, for farm and domestic workers, and for those who work for nonprofit organizations. There also are special rules for workers who are not covered by Social Security, as well as special guidelines for those claiming disability and survivor benefits. All this information can be found in SSA Publication 05-10072, *How You Earn Credits*. Request a copy at www.socialsecurity.gov or call 1-800-772-1213.

How Much Will You Get?

In October 1999, the SSA began mailing annual, individualized Social Security statements to workers 25 or older who were not yet getting Social Security benefits. Statements arrived in your mailbox each year about three months before your birth month. The statements contained a record of your earnings and estimates of your retirement and disability benefits.

Effective April 2011, this practice was suspended because of SSA budgetary constraints. In February 2012, the SSA resumed automatic mailing of the statements—but only to people age 60 and older who are not receiving monthly Social Security benefits. Beginning May 1, 2012, workers aged 18 and older can get their Social Security statements online. However, workers need to verify their identity before they can view their personalized statements. Workers who verify their identity correctly will receive a letter and an e-mail message acknowledging that they have created an account with the SSA. Workers who are unable to complete the verification process online have the option of verifying their identity in person at a local Social Security office and requesting that a paper Social Security statement be mailed to them.

Meanwhile in July 2012, the SSA began mailing "one time only" statements to workers in the year they turned age 25.

What does the statement tell you? Quite a lot, actually. It gives you an estimate of your benefits at age 62, at full retirement age, and at age 70. The age-62 estimate includes the reduction for early retirement; the age-70 estimate includes the credits given for delayed retirement. It also gives you an estimate of the amount of monthly disability benefit you could be entitled to and an estimate of the monthly benefit that your family could receive should you die.

What is your retirement benefit based on? Basically, Social Security retirement benefits are based on the amount of money you earned during your lifetime—with an emphasis on the 35 years in which you earned the most. This information is fed into SSA computers and subjected to several formulas that we discussed earlier.

Eventually, the SSA arrives at your basic benefit, or primary insurance amount (PIA). The PIA is what the agency considers to be your full retirement amount. The annual benefits statement should be of great help to people who are eager to know how much money they can expect to receive when they retire.

Conceivably, if this annual look ahead shows some individuals that their future benefits will be small, it could inspire these low-wage earners to increase their efforts to earn higher salaries in order to improve their chances of drawing higher retirement benefits.

Applying for Social Security Benefits

There are three basic ways to apply for Social Security retirement benefits. One is to apply online at www.socialsecurity.gov and click on "Applying Online for Retirement Benefits." The two other ways are to call the SSA and start the application process over the telephone or to ask for an appointment at your local Social Security office and apply in person.

The SSA's toll-free telephone number, 1-800-772-1213, operates 24 hours a day, including weekends and holidays. The phone reps are available from 7 a.m to 7 p.m. on business days. People who are deaf or hard of hearing can call a toll-free "TTY" number, 1-800-325-0778.

When you call to apply for retirement benefits, the phone rep will schedule a telephone interview for you. At that time, you will be asked a number of questions, and you will be requested to mail the originals of several important documents. Once the documents have been received by the SSA, they will be copied and returned to you.

If you would prefer to apply in person, the phone reps will make an appointment for you to visit your local SSA office. You also can use the toll-free line to inform the agency that you have changed your address or to arrange to have your monthly payments sent directly to your bank.

The information and documents you will need when you apply for retirement benefits generally include the following:

- Your Social Security number

- Your birth certificate

- Your W-2 forms or self-employment tax return for the previous year

- Your military discharge papers if you served in the armed forces

- Your spouse's birth certificate and Social Security number if he or she is also applying for benefits

- Proof of U.S. citizenship or lawful alien status if you (or a spouse who is applying for benefits) were not born in the United States

- The name of your bank and your account number so that your benefits can be deposited directly into your account

THE SPECIAL-PAYMENTS PROBLEM

Sometimes the best way to learn about a problem is to experience it. That's what happened to my wife and me. Sara retired in 1993, 2½ years before I did. As I recall, we each phoned the SSA and later visited our local office, bringing the required documents.

Dealing with the SSA was a relatively pleasant and low-key experience—at least until we ran into Sara's "special-payments" problem. That turned into a pretty confusing and nerve-wracking situation. Here's what happened.

Sara retired from General Electric on December 31, 1993, and began receiving Social Security benefits in February 1994. When Sara had applied for benefits several months earlier, she was asked what she expected to earn in 1994. Her answer was that she didn't expect to earn anything in 1994 because she was retiring and would not be working. However, when Sara retired, GE owed her $27,231 in severance pay and vacation pay, all related to her working years. Because she retired on December 31, that money was paid to Sara early in 1994 and was reported on our income taxes for 1994.

In August 1995, Sara received a letter from the SSA saying, in effect: You told us that you would not earn any money in 1994, but now we see that you reported earnings of $27,231. So, unless there are some things we don't know about, you have to give back $5,183 of your 1994 Social Security payments!

That letter sent Sara and me into overdrive, and after a flurry of phone calls and visits to our local SSA office, we finally discovered the problem: the agency did not know that the $27,231 represented severance and vacation pay that was due her for her work at GE before she retired.

That fact was important, because the SSA has a special set of rules that apply to payments of those kinds after you retire. Under these rules, Social Security does not count as earnings some types of "special payments" that you receive after you leave your job—if the payments are related to services that you provided to your company before you retired.

Sara was able to prove that she had not worked in 1994 by furnishing a letter from her employer that showed that the $27,231 came from severance pay, vacation pay, and other monies owed to her. The SSA agreed that these were, indeed, "special payments," so Sara did not have to return any of her Social Security benefits.

While the situation was resolved to our satisfaction, it left us with a few more gray hairs than we had had before. Several years later, when I retired from the *Washington Post* with my own severance and vacation pay package, I remembered Sara's experience. So I asked the newspaper to give me a letter showing what the payments that were made to me covered. I filed the letter with Social Security and thus managed to head off a demand that I return a chunk of my Social Security benefits. When you retire, watch out for this one!

RUNNING INTO THE EARNINGS LIMITS

At first, Sara and I didn't understand why Social Security even cared about whether she earned any money after she retired. It took us a while to figure out that Sara had run into the Social Security "earnings limits." In fact, she didn't work in 1994 or earn any money in any manner, but the SSA initially assumed that she had worked and had gone over the earnings limit.

In the course of clearing up the confusion, we learned that if retirees work and go over the earnings limit, they have to give back some of their benefits. The earnings limit affects those between 62 and full retirement age who receive Social Security benefits and continue to work.

In 2013, $1 in benefits is withheld for every $2 in earnings above the limit of $15,120. A different limit applies in the year in which you reach full retirement age. For people attaining full retirement age in 2013, $1 in benefits is deducted for every $3 in earnings above the limit of $40,080—but only until the month of your birthday. All this information can be found in SSA Publication 05-10069, *How Work Affects Your Benefits*. Request a copy at www.socialsecurity.gov or call 1-800-772-1213.

Worrying About the Future

When I retired and began to learn about Social Security, I had two main questions. The first was, how does Social Security work? In this chapter, I've tried to provide some basic answers to that question.

My second question was, will Social Security still be around when my children and grandchildren retire? It would take a separate book to explore all the aspects of that question. Indeed, many such books have been written. But on the basis of what we know now, Social Security seems to be financially secure for the "short term," which covers the next three decades.

The 2012 report from the Social Security and Medicare boards of trustees tells us that the Social Security trust funds are "adequately financed" until 2033. This means that until that year, there will be enough money coming into Social Security to pay 100 percent of the benefits due. After that, however, Social Security will begin to feel the effects of a shrinking workforce and a growing number of retirees. As the years go on, fewer and fewer workers will be contributing to the system, while more and more workers will retire and stop contributing.

Today, there are 35 beneficiaries taking money out of the Social Security pool for every 100 workers who are putting money in. In 2008, the year that the baby boomers began to retire, there were 31 beneficiaries receiving payments for every 100 workers. By 2034, that number will rise to 49 beneficiaries per 100 workers, and in 2075, it will go up to 51 beneficiaries per 100 workers.

Social Security is America's most popular federal income program. For 78 years, its monthly payments have provided a safety net for the aged, widowed, and disabled. In fact, two-thirds of all beneficiaries receive more than half of their income from Social Security. For millions of widows, it is their only income. Though Social Security has its flaws, it has been dependable in good times and bad.

Thus, it is no surprise that politicians call Social Security the "third rail of politics," meaning: "Don't touch it or you will get burned." But the national image of Social Security as a bastion of certainty has begun to erode, and Social Security finds itself at the center of a fierce political debate over its future. The reason for the struggle is quite simple. The retirement of 78 million baby boomers, which began in 2008 and will continue for two decades, is creating a stressful financial situation for the government. Social Security is a pay-as-you-go system: payroll taxes paid into the system by today's workers are used to provide benefits to today's retirees. This system worked well when there were many more workers putting money in than taking money out. But as the boomers retire, fewer and fewer workers will be contributing to Social Security, while more and more workers will leave the workforce and stop contributing.

Figure 3.1 shows the expected decline in the number of workers for each Social Security beneficiary. From 3.7 workers in 1970, the number dropped to 3.2 in 2008 and will drop sharply to 2.0 workers in 2075. What this means is that if no changes are made to the Social Security system, the 78-year-old program

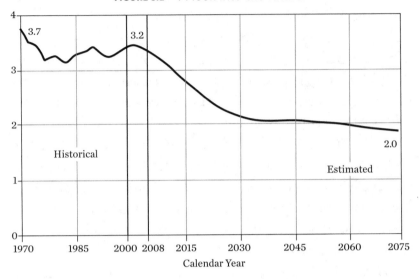

FIGURE 3.1 A look into the future.

Source: Social Security and Medicare Boards of Trustees, 2009 annual reports.

faces a dire future. The 2009 report from the Social Security and Medicare boards of trustees predicted the following:

- In 2010, taxes paid into Social Security fell short of the benefits paid out.

- In 2021, Social Security will have to start cashing in its government bonds to keep paying normal benefits.

- By 2033, those funds will run out.

After that, the payroll taxes being paid into Social Security will allow the agency to pay only 75 percent of its regular benefits. *And that will drop to 73.9 percent in 2083.*

What does all this mean for you and me? Since I am 86 and 2033 is 20 years away, my Social Security payments are likely to last at least as long as I do. However, unless Congress finds a way to shore up Social Security's finances, my children and grand-children will get much smaller payments than I am now getting.

My daughter, who was born in 1960, will reach her full retirement age of 67 in 2027. Thus, she would get full benefits for 6 years, until she was 73, and then would get partial benefits. My granddaughter, who was born in 1985, will reach her full retirement age of 67 in 2052, long after Social Security's assets have been depleted. Thus, she would get only partial benefits. And my other granddaughter, born in 1993, would reach 67 in 2060, when partial benefits would be moving toward 78.1 percent. Faced with these projections, Washington's politicians, lawmakers, and policy experts agree that action is needed to solve Social Security's long-range financial problem. But they differ on how to do that.

President George W. Bush proposed a plan to allow workers to divert a portion of their Social Security payroll taxes to personal investment accounts. In an effort to deal with the long-term solvency problem, Bush also proposed reducing Social Security benefits for middle- and upper-income people while protecting the benefits of low-income Americans. The benefit reduction, Bush said, would make up 70 percent of Social Security's long-term deficit.

Bush's proposals were supported by many Republican lawmakers, but were opposed by congressional Democrats, union leaders, and a number of public policy analysts. They argued that the so-called Social Security crisis was overblown and that, with minor fixes, the present system could remain solvent and continue to pay the scheduled benefits.

Ideas for solving Social Security's financial problems include raising the age for early retirement, which now begins at 62; shortening the 21-year period it will take for the full retirement age to move up from 65 to 67; raising the Social Security payroll tax to include wages above the current limit; and trimming retirement benefits for high-wage earners.

The personal accounts endorsed by Bush would have been voluntary and would have applied only to workers born in 1950 or later. Until recently , as explained earlier in this chapter, workers paid 6.2 percent of their wages to Social Security. Bush would have permitted workers to divert 4 percent of that money to personal investment accounts. The money could have been invested in stocks, bonds, or other financial assets. The personal accounts would have supplemented a much-reduced Social Security benefit, and the size of a worker's retirement account would have depended on how well his or her investments performed.

This debate over the future of Social Security generated unusual intensity from individuals and organizations on all sides of the issues. President Bush made personal accounts the cornerstone of his second-term agenda and barnstormed the country to win public backing for his plan, which he said would allow workers to own their own accounts and pass them along to their heirs. Bush supporters mounted vigorous campaigns to promote personal accounts.

Opponents of the Bush plan were equally vocal. They included the 35-million-member AARP, the nation's largest senior citizen lobby; labor unions; and public interest groups. They argued that the Bush plan would destroy the family insurance concept of Social Security. Under the banner of reform, they said, the Bush plan would result in 20 to 30 percent cuts in future benefits for upper- and middle-income workers, thus turning Social Security into a welfare program for the poor. They also claimed that letting workers invest their Social Security money in the stock market was too risky.

Democrats in Congress lined up solidly against the Bush plans. In fact, they declined to even discuss Social Security until Bush agreed to withdraw his plan for private accounts. Bush's second term ended without major changes in Social Security. And the 2008–2009 stock market crash reinforced the argument that allowing workers to put their Social Security savings into the financial markets was risky indeed.

During the early days of President Barack Obama's administration, the White House was heavily focused on its effort to win support for a national healthcare reform plan. That led it to put Social Security on the back burner. But the White House website made it clear that Obama was "committed to protecting Social Security." It also said, "The President stands firmly opposed to privatization and rejects the notion that the future of hard-working Americans should be left to the fluctuations of the financial markets."

President Obama's re-election in 2012 made it clear that he was determined to protect Social Security from legislative efforts to drastically change the way Social Security works. Even so, the future of Social Security will be at the center of a wide-ranging Washington debate over how to reduce government spending and increase federal revenues. That debate will also include the future of Medicare, as well.

For More Information

The SSA publishes a number of booklets that explain the agency's retirement programs. The booklets, which are free, are available at your local SSA office; on the agency's website, www.social security.gov; or by calling 1-800-772-1213.

The following booklets are recommended for present and future retirees:

Understanding the Benefits (Pub. 05-10024)
Retirement Benefits (Pub. 05-10035)
How Work Affects Your Benefits (Pub. 05-10069)
Your Retirement Benefit: How It Is Figured (Pub. 05-10070)

BOOKS

Berson, Susan A. *The Lawyer's Retirement Planning Guide.* Chicago: American Bar Association, 2010.

How Should I Take My Pension Payments?

Soon after I announced my retirement in the spring of 1996, I paid a visit to Michael C. Bahr, the benefits analyst in the *Washington Post's* personnel department. For more than 20 years, Mike shepherded hundreds of employees through the retirement process, helping them make crucial decisions on how to deal with both their pensions and their 401(k) savings plans. Mike always made time to answer my questions about *Post* benefits.

Over the years, Mike and I had often chatted about the ups and downs of the stock market and the mutual funds that were offered to employees who were enrolled in the newspaper's 401(k) savings plan. But I do not recall that we ever spent much time talking about the inner workings of the *Post's* pension plan.

For one thing, the idea that I'd retire someday had always seemed to me to be rather remote. Second, I had a sense that pension plans were very complicated, and I had no desire to strain my brain with information that I wouldn't need for quite a while. So I never asked Mike to explain how my *Post* pension would be calculated, although, looking back, I wish I had. It would have given me more time to think about my pension options before I retired.

Once a year, Mike sent each *Post* employee a report that showed how much pension money that employee could expect to receive when he or she reached age 65. I recall that each year, when I looked at the figures in my report, I would think to myself, "That's not enough money to live on," and I would dismiss the idea of retiring.

Indeed, one of the reasons I worked until I was 69 was because I hoped that additional years on the job and a rising pay level would help improve my pension when I finally decided to take it. And that's exactly what happened.

Understanding Your Pension Plan

There are, of course, two main types of pension plans: defined-benefit plans, which are paid for by the employer, and defined-contribution plans, such as 401(k) savings plans, to which the employee, and often the employer, contribute.

The *Post's* basic pension plan was a defined-benefit plan. The *Post* paid all the expenses; I put no money into it. The pension benefits I now receive were based on a formula that took into account several factors, including the total number of years I worked at the paper, my average salary during my five highest-paid years on the job, and the amount of money the company contributed to Social Security for me.

Using the *Post* formula, Mike figured out how much money I would get in my pension check each month if I took the maximum amount. He then told me I had several choices as to how I could take my monthly payments:

- A single life pension. This meant that I would receive my maximum pension of $2,532 a month, before deductions. But I could draw that pension check only during my lifetime. When I died, the pension would cease, and my wife would get nothing.

- A 50 percent spousal benefit. This meant that I could take a lower amount—about $2,160 a month for as long as I lived—but after my death, my wife would receive half of my check, or $1,080 a month.

- A 100 percent spousal benefit. This meant that I would take an even lower benefit—about $1,900 a month—but after my death, my wife would receive the same $1,900 check each month.

In other words, if I agreed to take less of a pension while I was alive, my spouse could continue to receive a pension check from the *Post* for as long as she lived.

MAKING THE PENSION DECISION

The question facing us was this: was it better—from both a financial and a common sense point of view—to take my full pension or to take either the 50 percent or 100 percent spousal benefit? At the time I retired, Sara was already retired. And we were concerned that it might be difficult for us to go from living on two full salaries to living on a combination of pensions and Social Security income. Understandably, we felt that we would like to go into retirement with as much monthly income as possible.

This wasn't just a matter of greed. As I noted in an earlier chapter, I hadn't given much thought to my retirement budget. And it didn't look as if our monthly living expenses would go down much when we retired. In fact, it seemed as if they might go up. In short, because we hadn't planned carefully for our retirement budget, it seemed that we would need all the income we could get.

There were other factors, too. Sara, who had retired about two years earlier, was getting a pension of about $700 a month from GE. I also had more than $200,000 in life insurance. Our idea was that if I died, Sara could invest the insurance money at a 6 percent interest rate and receive an annual income of $12,000, or $1,000 a month. That seemed like a good idea at the time, but $100,000 of my insurance consisted of a term life policy that eventually ran out and was too expensive to hang on to. Also, in the wake of the 2008–2009 market crash and recession, investing money at a 6 percent rate now seems like a distant dream. Fortunately, we both had modest 401(k) rollover accounts that she could draw on if I died.

But based on our original strategy at the time, it seemed to us that Sara would be protected financially if I took my maximum pension and left her no *Post* pension. So we did it. Sara signed off on the deal—something that she was required to do by law. The federal government wants to be sure people are aware that if their spouses take a single life pension, they can be left without any pension income.

HAVING SECOND THOUGHTS

It is, of course, far too late for me to change my decision, although I must tell you that I am still, many years later, having some second thoughts about the idea of taking my maximum pension payment and not leaving any pension for Sara. My second thoughts began to arise shortly after I retired when I decided to figure out how our family income would change upon my death. I added up how much money we were getting from pensions and Social Security. The total from pensions (after tax was withheld and after other deductions) was then $2,893. The total from Social Security was $2,600. The grand total was $5,493 a month.

But see how the picture would have changed if I had died.

First, Sara would lose her $1,355 Social Security payment and get mine instead, because mine is higher. So she would get $2,123 a month from Social Security. Add her GE pension of $801 (after tax is withheld and after other deductions), and her grand total would be $2,932.

That's a big difference. In fact, it was a $3,685 difference between what we got together and what she'd get alone—a drop of 56 percent. How much income she could have received from my remaining $100,000 of life insurance and our 401(k) investments was problematical.

Sara's living expenses, as a single person, might be somewhat lower than they were for the two of us together. But I think Sara's comfort level would have been higher if she knew she would receive my pension for the rest of her life. Moreover, she wouldn't have had to spend a lot of time managing investments or depending on others to do it for her. Nor would she have had to worry about the health of the financial markets and whether her nest egg was being eroded.

So, after thinking about it, I have come to the conclusion that Sara would have been better off if I had taken the 100 percent spousal benefit. That would have given me a monthly check of $1,900, and she would have continued to get the same check after I died. It would have been costly, of course; we would have given up $632 a month, and that would have made it harder for us to pay our bills. But it might have had advantages in future years.

Trying to Outguess Life

There is, of course, no way to know how long we are going to live; hence, speculating about what might happen in the future has its limitations. But let's try it, anyway.

Let's say that when I retired at 69, I took the 100 percent spousal benefit of $1,900 a month. And let's say that I lived for 10 years after retirement. By taking the $1,900 check instead of the full $2,532, I would have lost $632 a month, or $7,584 a year, or $75,840 for those 10 years.

However, if Sara survived me for another 4 years, she would have gotten the same $1,900 a month check. That would add up to $22,800 a year, or $91,200 over those four years. So we would have more than broken even. In addition, Sara would have had the security of knowing that she was getting a regular pension check. And I think that's important.

Perhaps if I had thought all this through more carefully before I retired, I might have made a different decision on how to take my pension. The point of this story, though, is that the decision regarding how to take your pension is not a simple one. It has many more dimensions than I realized at the time I retired—and many more dimensions than you might realize.

Every pension plan is somewhat different. Therefore, every plan will have different options. For instance, the *Washington Post* plan did not offer a lump-sum option. But many pension plans do. Thus, you may have to choose between taking your pension in one lump sum or in monthly payments.

That lump-sum option has some pros and cons, which are summarized next.

TAKING A LUMP-SUM PAYMENT

Pro

Taking a lump sum enables you to make your own decisions on how you want to invest your money. As a result, you may be able to earn a higher income from your investments than you would get from a monthly pension check. The money also would be available for an emergency or a business opportunity. Finally, monthly pension checks end when you die or when your spouse dies. But the lump-sum money, if wisely invested, would still be there for your heirs.

Cons

The temptation to spend all or some of your lump-sum money may be overwhelming. That's what happens to many people who get large amounts of money in lump-sum payments. A full 40 percent of workers aged 55 to 64 spend all or some of their lump-sum money, according to the U.S. Department of Labor. The other 60 percent put all their pension money into savings—a move that will help them pay for their living expenses in retirement. Moreover, the job of managing a large sum of money may involve more investment risk than you are either used to or comfortable with. And though you could derive more income from investing your money yourself, you also could get less if the investment climate is unfavorable. In addition, your lump-sum payment is likely to be fully taxable, which would give you a large tax bite in one year and thus reduce the amount of money you have available to invest. However, you can postpone the taxes due on your lump-sum payment by rolling over the entire amount into an IRA. The money then can continue to grow on a tax-deferred basis until you are ready to take it out.

TAKING A MONTHLY PAYMENT

Pros

The process is simple: once you've decided which option to choose—single life or a spousal benefit—the rest is automatic. You know how much you'll be getting each month, making it easy for you to draw up your retirement budget and to plan for taxes. Gyrations in the stock market or the bond market won't be a worry, since your income is set. And if you're lucky enough to have a long retirement, those monthly payments will add up.

Cons

Pension plans generally are not adjusted for inflation. Thus, you could steadily lose purchasing power over the years. At an inflation rate of 3 percent, you would lose half your purchasing power in 24 years. And once you've taken your pension as a monthly payment—also called an annuity—you can't change it. Furthermore, your pension ends when you die or when your spouse dies. That means that there won't be any pension money to leave to your heirs.

In any event, Mike Bahr of the *Post* helped me put together a list of the things that a future retiree should think about before making pension decisions:

- Talk to the benefits expert in your company and ask for an explanation of the formula that your pension plan uses to determine how much money you will get when you retire. It may be possible to schedule your retirement in a way that will help you get a larger benefit. If, for instance, you expect a sizable pay raise in the next two years, it might be worth staying on the job to boost your average pay history—which could raise the amount of your pension.

- When talking to the benefits expert, get a copy of the various monthly payment options that will be available to you. Take time to study them, and think about the implications of giving up income now in order to provide income for your spouse in the future.

- Remember that your pension is considered by the IRS to be income and thus is fully taxable. Most pension plans will withhold taxes if you request that option. But, of course, tax withholding and deductions for health or life insurance will reduce the amount of money you will get in each check. Thus, in planning your retirement budget, use your net pension amount, not your gross amount.

- If you decide to take a lump-sum payment and roll it over into an IRA, make sure that the rollover is made directly to the mutual fund, brokerage firm, or other company that you choose for your IRA account. The most efficient way is to have your employer send the money directly to the company that will be handling your account. That avoids taxes and penalties.

If you tell your employer to give you the money first—called an *indirect rollover*—the employer will withhold 20 percent for taxes, and you will have 60 days to open the IRA account, at which time you will have to make up the 20 percent from your own pocket. While you can get the 20 percent back eventually, you'll have to file a tax form to do so. So spare yourself that hassle by doing a direct rollover. Make the arrangements with your company and the institution that you choose for your IRA in advance.

- Before making any final decisions, consider the state of your health and that of your spouse. If you or your spouse has health problems that may shorten your normal longevity, consider those factors when making your pension choices.

- Consider, too, your overall financial situation, and try to choose a pension option that best fits that situation. If you take the maximum pension, as I did, will your spouse have enough other income coming in—or savings to draw on—to make ends meet when your pension stops? If you have limited savings and you need Social Security and pension income to support you, you may want to make sure that your spouse continues to get a pension check after your death, even if you have to take a lower monthly payment to do so.

- Think about your family obligations. Are there children or other relatives who depend on you for financial help? Those obligations may influence your decision regarding which pension payment option to take.

Finding a Lost Pension

Ordinarily, when you decide to retire and take your pension, all you need to do is walk down the hall at work and talk to the benefits person. But suppose that after you've done that, you remember that 25 years ago you left a smaller company that also had a pension plan. Now that you're retiring, you wonder if you're entitled to a pension from your previous employer.

So you decide to call the company. You look in the phone book. The company is not listed. You call directory assistance. It doesn't have a listing either. You call the chamber of commerce. None of its people have ever heard of the company. You do an Internet search. You try everything you can think of, but you can't find the company.

It doesn't seem that it would be that easy for a company to disappear. But it happens all the time, especially in this era of mergers and acquisitions. According to the Pension Benefit Guaranty Corporation (PBGC), a federal agency, "Thousands of retired workers in the United States are entitled to pension payments that they have not claimed because they do not know where to look."

As the PBGC points out in its useful booklet *Finding a Lost Pension*, a company may:

- Move from one town to another.

- Close a plant and consolidate its operations elsewhere.

- Be bought by another company and given a new name.

- Merge with another company.

- Divide into separate units, none of which keeps the original company name.

- Go bankrupt.

- Close its doors and go out of business.

But even if a company has disappeared, that doesn't mean that the company's pension plan has also disappeared. In many cases, the PBGC says, the money is sitting safely in a fund somewhere, waiting for the worker, or perhaps a surviving spouse, to come forward and claim it.

Helping people find "missing pensions" is one of the many responsibilities of the PBGC. The federal agency was created by the Employee Retirement Income Security Act of 1974 (ERISA) to encourage the continuation of defined-benefit pension plans, provide timely and uninterrupted payment of pension benefits, and keep pension insurance premiums at a minimum. Currently, PBGC insurance protects the retirement benefits of 44 million workers. Because of that insurance, these workers will get their pensions even if their employer goes out of business or the plan runs out of money.

The PBGC's Pension Search program may help you locate a "missing" pension. However, there are a couple of things you need to think about before you start looking. A key question is, "Were you vested in the company's pension plan before you left the company?" Being vested means that no matter when you leave a job, you are eligible to receive a pension when you retire. If you weren't vested, you may not have a chance to claim benefits.

Today, most pension plans require 5 years of employment before vesting. Prior to the mid-1980s, plans typically required 10 years of service to vest. Prior to the mid-1970s, they usually required 20 years.

Also, before 1976, to get a pension, you could be required to work for the same employer until you actually retired.

Indeed, from 1952 to 1971, I worked for a company in which you joined the pension plan at age 30, but you did not vest and thus could not get your pension until you retired at age 65, some 35 years later. If you left the company anytime before age 65, you got your own contributions back, plus 3 percent interest. And so, when I left the company at the age of 44, I lost about 14 years of pension benefits. Under ERISA, that type of plan is no longer permitted.

ERISA also created other broad protections that help to prevent workers from losing their pensions. The Department of Labor monitors pension plans to make sure that they are solvent and are being managed properly. The Internal Revenue Service also regulates pension plans.

As mentioned earlier, the fact that a company has vanished doesn't mean that its pension plan has vanished, too. Many things could have happened to the plan. The PBGC notes that:

- Despite reorganizations and mergers, the original plan may be intact. Those who run what today is left of the old company may still have a legal obligation to pay benefits due under the old plan.

- The plan may have bought an annuity from an insurance company, which took on the obligation to pay annuities to everyone entitled to benefits under the plan.

- The plan may have been taken over by the PBGC, which will pay benefits up to certain limits.

- If the plan was terminated by the employer and benefits were paid to those employees who could be found, benefits for "missing" participants may have been turned over to the PBGC for its Pension Search program.

So it may be possible for you to find your missing pension after all. However, it may take quite a bit of research. Suggestions on how to conduct a search for a missing pension are contained in the PBGC publication *Finding a Lost Pension*. For a free copy, write to Pension Benefit Guaranty Corporation, Communications and Public Affairs Department, 1200 K St., NW, Washington, DC 20005-4026. The information is also available on the Internet at www.pbgc.gov; on the home page, click on "About," and the "About" page will give you a choice of "PBGC Publications."

The PBGC's website also allows you to search electronically for a "missing" pension on the PBGC web page, www.pbgc.gov. You can search for your own name, for the company name, or by state. Click on the "Find My Plan" button, then click the "Find Missing Participants" button.

For More Information

The following organizations can provide more information about pensions.

The U.S. Department of Labor. This agency's website offers information on pensions and other matters of interest to retirees (www.dol.gov).

The Employee Benefit Research Institute (EBRI). A research and education group, the EBRI seeks to enhance the development of sound employee benefit programs (www.ebri.org).

American Savings Educational Council (ASEC). A coalition of public- and private-sector institutions, the ASEC promotes savings and retirement planning (www.choosetosave.org/asec/).

AARP. The nation's largest organization for retirees and pre-retirees, AARP has a website that contains a wide range of pension-related information (www.aarp.org/research).

What Should I Do with the Money in My Company Savings Plan?

During the years that I worked at the *Washington Post*, I participated in the paper's 401(k) savings plan. This type of plan, offered by many U.S. companies, was created by Uncle Sam to encourage American workers to save for retirement and other financial goals.

These plans vary from company to company, but here is how the plan worked at the *Post*.

As an employee, I set aside a portion of my salary for savings—we were paid every two weeks—and the paper automatically deposited that money into my account. In my later years at the paper, I put about 9 percent of my pay into the 401(k) account.

The savings plan had several great features. To begin with, the amount of money that I earmarked for savings was deducted from my pay before my income taxes were calculated and withheld. That reduced my taxable earnings each payday and thus also reduced my income taxes for the year. So, in a sense, I was doing two things at once: saving money regularly and also saving on income taxes. I thought that was a pretty good deal.

But it got even better. After I made my regular contribution to the savings plan, the *Post* put in its contribution, called a *company match*. In my later years at the paper, as long as I made the requisite contribution to my account, the company contributed another 4.5 percent of my pay, or about half of my contribution.

Finally, the paper gave me several choices as to how I wanted to invest the money in my account. I studied the list of available funds and decided to put my contributions into the Vanguard Windsor mutual fund, one of several stock funds that were offered to *Post* employees. I also decided to use the company's matching money to buy *Washington Post* stock.

Over the years, I have become convinced that a 401(k) plan is a powerful way to save for retirement. It has several major advantages:

- Your contribution goes directly into your savings plan before it is taxed. Thus, 100 cents of every dollar that you put into the plan goes to work. The contribution also reduces your income taxes for that year.

- The company's matching contribution is "free money." It's yours as long as you contribute enough to receive it (a vesting schedule may apply). It increases the amount of dollars that you have in your account. Those dollars also grow on a tax-deferred basis.

- Many companies let you invest your tax-deferred savings in mutual funds. That means that your money will be managed by investment professionals who are likely to be able to make your money grow over a period of years. Essentially, your money makes money—the wonderful bit of arithmetic called *compounding* that was so admired by Professor Albert Einstein, as noted in Decision 2.

- No taxes are due on your savings or on any of the gains in your 401(k) plan until you begin to withdraw the money. However, as mentioned earlier, when you take out money that has not been taxed before, it will be taxed at ordinary income tax rates. In my case, I began to take money out of my account when I turned 70½, as required by the IRS. We'll talk about how to make your withdrawals in Decision 6.

Looking back, I can see that being able to participate in the *Post*'s 401(k) plan for many years made a significant difference in the amount of money I had available for my retirement years. The same was true for Sara, who saved her money in a 401(k) plan at GE.

My gratitude for our 401(k) plans, however, does not change the warning I issued in Decision 2 about the impact of taxes on retirees. While people should take maximum advantage of the 401(k) plan, they should also be aware that after they retire and begin to take money out of their tax-deferred savings accounts, they will pay income taxes on those withdrawals. They should set aside money to pay those taxes.

As Sara and I discovered, the tax bite can be rather large. Early in my retirement, it even became difficult for us to balance our family budget. I simply hadn't realized how much I would owe in taxes after taking money out of our 401(k) rollover accounts.

As mentioned earlier, if your income from pensions and Social Security totals $40,000 a year and you withdraw $10,000 from your IRAs, your total income will rise to $50,000. That is likely to increase your taxes for that year. Remember, however, that only a portion—up to 85 percent—of your Social Security benefits can be taxed each year.

Despite the tax aspect, Sara and I urge anyone who has the opportunity to contribute to a retirement savings plan at work to do so. Sign up as soon as you're eligible. Put in as much money into the plan as you can afford, up to the limit allowed by the plan. And in the year you reach your fiftieth birthday, begin making "catch-up" contributions as well. If you are lucky, your plan will also include a new opportunity—namely, the ability to contribute after-tax dollars to a Roth 401(k) account instead of making pretax contributions to the traditional 401(k) account. (You can contribute to one or both, but the combined total cannot exceed IRS limits.)

As you may know, there are no income eligibility limits for contributing to a Roth 401(k), although there are limits for contributing to a regular Roth IRA. In the past, there have been income limits for conversions of traditional IRAs to Roth IRAs, but those limits went away in 2010.

So if you are concerned about possible increased taxes after you are retired, you may want to convert some or all of the assets in your traditional IRAs to Roth IRAs and, if possible, pay the taxes due with assets that you hold in a taxable investment account. The main advantage of converting is that thereafter you won't have to withdraw funds from your Roth IRAs unless you want to, since no required minimum distributions (RMDs) are applied, and when you do withdraw funds, you won't have to pay income taxes on those withdrawals. And the withdrawals by your beneficiaries someday, which can be stretched out over a long period of time in many cases, will be tax-free as well.

Turning Workers into Investors

For Sara and me, the 401(k) plan made it easy for us to save regularly and automatically year after year.

In the days before we had our 401(k) plans, we would take each paycheck and try to carve out a small piece for our savings account. Depending on how many bills we had on our desk, the money would sometimes get into our savings account and sometimes not.

With the advent of the 401(k) plan, our savings efforts were put on automatic pilot. The money came out of our paychecks regularly and silently, and it was difficult and potentially costly to access. We also got the benefit of matching money from our employers and tax deferral from Uncle Sam.

That's the good news about contributing to a 401(k) plan. The bad news—if you want to call it that—is that once you put money into a plan, you also have to decide how you want to invest it. That sounds like it ought to be easy, but it's not: making your own investment decisions can be a considerable responsibility, especially as your nest egg grows over the years.

For instance, let's assume that you earned $50,000 a year and put 6 percent of your salary ($250 a month) into your 401(k) plan. Your employer then matched half of your contribution with another $125 a month. That made the total contribution $375 a month.

Let's also assume that you invested your savings in a Standard & Poor's (S&P) 500 index mutual fund for 20 years—namely, the decades of the 1980s and 1990s. During that period of time, the S&P 500's average annual total return was 11.2 percent a year, with dividends and capital gains reinvested. Thus, by the end of the 20 years, your 401(k) plan would have accumulated $333,332, less the expenses of the index fund.

My point is that people who may have known little about investing can wake up one day and find themselves with extremely large amounts of money in their 401(k) plans, simply because they were fortunate enough to have steady, well-paying jobs for 15 or 20 years or more during an era when the financial markets provided solid returns.

On the other hand, the markets do not always treat investors so favorably. After the financial tsunami of 2008–2009, market watchers began talking about "the lost decade" for stocks. They noted that as of the end of April 2009, the 10-year annualized return on the S&P 500 index was negative 2.5 percent. In other words, if you had invested in the S&P 500 in 1999 and hadn't contributed anything since, when you looked at your investment 10 years later, you would have lost money.

While that kind of statistic can be discouraging, it also reminds investors that they have to choose their investments carefully and monitor them over the years. It also highlights another benefit of automatic savings.

Meanwhile, thanks mainly to the 401(k) plan, the reality is that millions of American workers who otherwise might never have owned a stock or even a mutual fund are now "in the market" and have a stake in the performance of individual companies and the ups and downs of the financial markets. Those of us in the financial media—print, radio, and television—have seen an incredible growth in the audience for news and information about financial markets.

Of course, while investing in stocks and bonds offers you a chance to share in the long-term growth of the American economy, it also forces you to share in the market's short-term gyrations. On Wall Street, traders are fond of saying, "The market climbs a wall of worry." Individual investors, too, often have to climb that same wall. One of the great challenges of long-term investing is to learn enough about the markets and how they operate to be able to make intelligent investment decisions. We'll talk more about that in Decision 7.

Meanwhile, I can testify that even people with knowledge of investing can act emotionally and make serious mistakes with their 401(k) money. I know because I did exactly that. This is my story.

MY $70,000 INVESTMENT MISTAKE

In the 1980s, I was investing my 401(k) money in the Windsor Fund, a value-oriented stock mutual fund that was part of the Vanguard Group. The Windsor Fund was one of the investment choices offered to *Post* employees. The fund provided a respectable return. During the six years I was in it, it gained an average of 11.8 percent a year, and my savings grew nicely.

But in 1990, I got very nervous about the safety of my nest egg. On August 2, Iraq invaded Kuwait, and the international scene became very unsettled. I thought that a war might be in the offing. The markets also became very volatile. The Dow Jones Industrial Average dropped 18 percent between August 1 and October 11, 1990, on fears that the United States might get into a Middle East battle. At the same time, the price of the shares in the Windsor Fund fell from $12.39 to $9.72, a drop of 22 percent.

I was dismayed by the loss in value of my Windsor shares and concerned about whether the downdraft would get worse. So I sold my shares and moved my money to a Vanguard money market fund. As it turned out, that was a bad mistake. In January 1991, when U.S. bombers struck Baghdad and returned without meeting significant resistance, the U.S. stock market came roaring back. The Dow ended 1991 with a gain of 20 percent, and the Windsor Fund rose 28.6 percent. By leaving the fund when I did, I got the fund's losses, and I wasn't there to get any of the fund's gains when the price of a share went back up.

That, unfortunately, is not the end of the story. Because of inertia or just a failure to pay attention to my financial affairs, I left my money in the money market fund for the next 5½ years until I retired. During those years, the money market fund earned a paltry (at that time!) average of 4.6 percent a year, while the Windsor Fund turned in an annualized gain of 18 percent a year.

I now figure that my decision to move my money out of the stock fund and into the money market fund—and leave it there for 5½ years—cost me about $70,000. True, it was money that I never actually had in my pocket. But if I had left the money in the Windsor Fund, I would have retired with an extra $70,000.

Naturally, my wife and friends wanted to know how a financial writer who was knowledgeable about the markets could make that kind of mistake. I don't have a good answer. But I did learn a valuable lesson: don't try to outguess the market. Decide on your long-term investment strategy, and as long as it's the right strategy for you, stick to it.

THE EDUCATED INVESTOR

When several of my friends heard about my $70,000 investment mistake, they tried to console me by confessing that they had made similar errors. "I know how you feel," they said. "I did the same thing myself." Frankly, it wasn't much consolation, but it was a reminder that millions of American workers are being called upon to make important investment decisions, often without much investment knowledge or experience.

Fortunately, a new national effort to expand "financial literacy" programs is under way across the country. The objective is to teach millions of citizens how to manage and invest their money so that they can provide financial security for themselves and members of their family.

In 2008, President Bush created a President's Advisory Council on Financial Literacy, accompanied by an executive order declaring it to be "the policy of the federal government to encourage financial literacy among the American people."

Mr. Bush asked the 16-member council, headed by investment executive Charles R. Schwab, to help public and private organizations develop financial education programs for students and workers in U.S. industries.

The White House recognition of the need to increase financial literacy was a pat on the back for several national organizations that have been working for many years to bring financial education to high schools and colleges.

In the council's first annual report, Schwab wrote:

We believe the market turmoil and credit crisis of 2008 underscore the critical need for improved financial literacy in the United States. . . . Far too many Americans entered into home and other loan agreements that they did not understand and ultimately could not afford. More broadly, the lack of basic skills such as how to create and maintain a budget, understand credit, or save for the future are preventing millions of Americans from taking advantage of our vibrant economic system.

On January 29, 2010, President Obama signed an executive order creating the President's Advisory Council on Financial Capability (PACFC). The Obama council essentially built on the objectives of the Bush council. Mr. Obama said, "Financial capability empowers individuals to make informed choices, avoid pitfalls, know where to go for help, and take other actions to improve their present and long-term financial well-being." John W. Rogers Jr. was named chairman of the PACFC. Mr. Rogers is the CEO of Ariel Investments, a Chicago-based mutual fund company.

Choosing What to Do with Your Money When You Retire

When you walk into the office of the benefits specialist at your company and announce that you are ready to retire, the specialist will tell you that you have several options for what to do with the money you have saved in your 401(k) plan.

If you have worked for 20 years or more, and you have been saving aggressively and investing thoughtfully, the amount in your savings account may be the largest pot of money you've ever had. If that is the case—and I hope it is—you will want to consider your options very carefully. Assuming that you are over 59½, those options include the following.

A ROLLOVER IRA

This is the option that Sara and I both chose when we retired. Before Sara left GE, she opened an IRA rollover account at a major mutual fund company. At that time, GE sent her a check for her 401(k) money that was made out both to her and to the mutual fund company (which indicated that the money had to go into her account at the fund company). Sara quickly took the check to the local office of the fund company and deposited the money into her account.

If she were doing it today, she'd fill out the paperwork requesting a "trustee-to-trustee transfer" and avoid the need to be the middleman. Initially, she parked the money in a money market account. Afterward, she studied the available mutual funds and invested portions of her money in some of those funds. Her objective was to keep the money invested and to keep it working and growing.

When I retired from the *Post* a few years later, I did much the same thing. I opened an IRA rollover account at a major brokerage firm, and the *Post* sent me a check for my 401(k) money made out both to me and to the brokerage company. I then deposited the check in my new rollover account, also initially in a money market fund. I chose a brokerage account because I wanted to invest in specific stocks rather than funds.

Over the past few years, I have had my share of winners and losers in the stock market, but, like Sara, I achieved my main purpose, which was to keep the money invested and growing.

What happens to our savings is of great concern to us because we know we will have to depend on our 401(k) money to help pay for some of our retirement expenses in the years ahead.

Doing a rollover IRA, I believe, was the best way to deal with our 401(k) money. But there are other options as well. A word of caution: if, despite recent market events, you have a significant amount of highly appreciated company stock in your retirement plan portfolio, you may wish to take advantage of a special tax break that is available to you. This is described in detail later in this chapter.

INDIRECT ROLLOVER IRA

In this scenario, your employer sends you a check made out just to you for your 401(k) money. However, your employer is required to withhold 20 percent of your money for income taxes—money that gets sent to the IRS. For instance, if you have $200,000 in your account, your employer will withhold $40,000 for the IRS and send you a check for $160,000. You will then have 60 days to open an IRA rollover account somewhere and deposit your money.

To avoid income taxes, you will be required to deposit the full $200,000 in your IRA rollover account. That means that you will have to come up with the $40,000 your employer withheld for taxes out of your own pocket. If you don't, this amount will be treated as a taxable distribution. Eventually, you may be able to get your $40,000 back when you file your federal income tax return for the year of the distribution.

In short, the indirect rollover produces the same result as the direct rollover, but it comes with a lot of hassle for very little gain. About the only benefit of this strategy is that you have the use of 80 percent of the money from your employer's plan for a maximum of 60 days. Under most circumstances, it hardly seems worth the trouble.

Whether you roll over your assets directly or indirectly into an IRA, the money in your 401(k) plan represents the money you and your employer put there, plus any gains on your investments. These sums are considered pretax money, meaning money that has yet to be taxed. However, if you contributed any additional money to your company account—money on which you have already paid taxes—it, too, may be rolled over into an IRA, or you may choose to take those assets and keep them in a taxable account for emergencies.

A CASH DISTRIBUTION

Taking all your savings out of your plan without rolling them over into an IRA is probably the worst thing you can do with your 401(k) money because you will simply give up most of it in taxes. Here is an example of what can happen to your $200,000 if you take it all in cash:

- First, your company will withhold 20 percent for taxes, or $40,000 for the IRS.

- Second, let's assume that the cash distribution puts you in the 33 percent marginal income tax bracket. Your employer has already withheld 20 percent. So you could owe another 13 percent of $200,000, or $26,000, if you withdraw the lump sum in one year.

- Third, in addition to paying federal taxes, you will have to remit state and/or local taxes on your withdrawal. Suppose that these taxes cost you another $10,000.

That all adds up to $76,000, leaving you only $124,000 from your original $200,000. That doesn't sound like a good way to handle money that you have carefully saved over so many years.

But perhaps the most devastating effect of taking a cash distribution is that all of your remaining money loses its tax-deferred status and becomes fully taxable, which can be costly over the long term. The dramatic difference between what a tax-deferred $200,000 will produce and what a taxable $124,000 will produce over long periods of time is shown in Table 5.1.

TABLE 5.1 Why It's Not a Good Idea to Take Your 401(k) Money in Cash

TIME PERIOD	GROWTH OF $200,000 ROLLOVER INVESTMENT (PRETAX BALANCES) *	GROWTH OF $124,000 CASH INVESTMENT (AFTER-TAX BALANCES)
10 years	$358,170	$183,550
15 years	$479,312	$223,317
20 years	$641,427	$271,699

*The rollover account will grow on a tax-deferred basis and assumes an average annual return of 6 percent. The after-tax lump sum is assumed to grow at an after-tax return of 4 percent.

Source: T. Rowe Price

Leaving Money in Your 401(k) Plan

Some 401(k) plans will permit you to leave your money in the plan; others will not. Federal regulations say that a company may make you roll over your assets into an IRA if you have less than $5,000 in your account when you leave the company. In many cases, I am told, you can stay in your plan if you have at least $5,000 there. Since your decision to leave your employer's plan will be irrevocable, it is important that you consult with a financial advisor before making your decision.

If you happen to be someone who plans to continue working part-time in a profession like medicine, where you are more likely to be exposed to litigation, you might want to leave your assets in the plan, as they may be better protected from your creditors than they would be if they were held in an IRA. This varies from state to state, so check with your attorney if you are concerned. Fees might be lower if you leave your assets in the plan. And in rare cases, you may continue to have opportunities to take loans from your account, even after you have left your employment. Finally, if you intend to continue working for your company after age 70½ and you do not own 5 percent or more of the company, you will probably be able to delay taking required minimum distributions from your plan account until the year after you finally retire. (If you have rolled over the assets into an IRA, however, required minimum distributions are mandatory even if you continue employment with your old employer.)

DEALING WITH COMPANY STOCK

If your 401(k) plan allowed you to invest in company stock, you have several options. You can sell the stock within your 401(k) plan, if that is permitted, and roll the total amount of money from your plan into an IRA rollover account, either directly or indirectly. Or, you can keep the shares of stock and roll them over into an IRA account, along with any other money in your plan.

However, you may have company stock in your plan that has substantially increased in value over the years. (Indeed, let's hope you do!) If so, to benefit from special tax treatment, you may want to consider moving the stock to a taxable brokerage account at the same time you roll over the balance of your 401(k) into an

IRA, suggests senior financial planner Christine S. Fahlund at T. Rowe Price Investment Services.

To be eligible for this special tax treatment, your one-time distribution from your employer plan must qualify as a lump-sum distribution, so be sure to check with your plan administrator before taking action.

This strategy enables you to pay capital gains taxes on the appreciation when you sell your company stock. The capital gains taxes may be considerably lower than the amount you would have to pay in ordinary income taxes when you withdraw assets from your rollover IRA account during retirement. The details get a bit tricky, but stay with me.

At the time the shares are taken from your 401(k) plan, you will pay ordinary income taxes only on the original cost basis of the shares, not on their fair market value. If you decide to sell some of the shares that you deposit in the brokerage account right away, you will pay long-term capital gains taxes (at a 0 or 15 percent rate in 2012) on the total long-term gains realized, since the shares were purchased in the plan. However, before selling shares of the stock that have appreciated further since that deposit date, you should hold those shares in the brokerage account for at least an additional year. The reason for applying this holding strategy is to avoid having those new gains treated as short-term and taxed at ordinary income tax rates, which would be higher.

If you never sell the shares, the tax advantages get even better, Fahlund says. This is what would happen: when your heirs sell the shares, they will not pay capital gains tax on any gains that occurred between the time you moved the shares to the brokerage account and the date of your death. That is because when you die, the cost basis of the shares is "stepped up," as tax people like to say. This means that for your heirs, the cost basis of your shares will usually be the price of the shares on the day you died. Thus, if they sell the shares immediately, they will pay capital gains taxes only on the appreciation that occurred while the shares were still in your 401(k) account.

All in all, the 401(k) plan is like a good friend. It'll be there when you need it. But as with any friend, take the time to get to know it well, and treat it with respect.

Saving in America: Good News and Bad

The good news is that the personal savings rate in America, after being negative for many years, rose to 6.9 percent in May 2009, the highest point in 15 years. Since then, the savings rate has declined, and in May 2012 it stood at 3.9 percent.

Even so, the bad news is that many people are now saving for the following reasons:

- The 2008–2009 market crash erased $2 trillion from workers' retirement savings.

- The national unemployment rate rose to almost 10 percent, with almost 15 million Americans out of work. In the fall of 2012, the unemployment rate was 8.2 percent, and millions of people were still unemployed.

- Because of the housing bust, home values plummeted, leaving many homeowners "underwater"—that is, owing more on their mortgages than their houses are worth.

- Because of job losses and falling home prices, millions of Americans lost their homes to foreclosure.

- The national business recession and "jobless recovery" extended through 2012 and beyond.

Simply put, Americans seem to be saving out of a fear of spending any money that they don't have to spend. The national recession and personal financial losses also affected the way baby boomers are thinking about their futures. An AARP study showed that 27 percent of all workers age 45 and older decided to postpone their plans to retire.

Under the circumstances, delaying retirement made sense for many boomers. At 65, they will become eligible for Medicare. If they left their jobs before they reached 65 and lost their company insurance, they might have had to pay privately for health insurance.

Also, by working past what Social Security calls your "full retirement age" (66 for most people who are retiring now), they earn an 8 percent bonus for each year that they delay taking Social Security benefits, plus any adjustment for inflation. At 70, they get a 32 percent bonus and are thus able to collect their maximum monthly Social Security payment. Conversely, their benefit is reduced if they start taking it before they turn 66.

Also, staying on the job allows the boomers to continue to draw their salaries and put money into their 401(k) plans for a few more years. That also might give their 401(k) investments time to recover from some of their losses.

If there is any irony to be found in the sudden boom in the national savings rate, it is that it follows years of surveys showing that American workers are not saving enough and are financially ill prepared for retirement. In the 2012 Retirement Confidence Survey conducted by the Employee Benefit Research Institute (EBRI) and Mathew Greenwald & Associates, 60 percent of those surveyed said that their savings and investments totaled less than $25,000, not counting the value of their homes or future pensions. Even more alarming, perhaps, 70 percent of workers said that their savings and investments totaled less than $50,000. And many of these workers were only a few years from retirement age.

Whether the current surge in the national savings rate will continue is uncertain, but, as of this writing, people who are trying hard to save for retirement are facing extraordinary financial challenges.

For More Information

BOOKS

Larimore, Taylor, Mel Lindauer, and Michael LeBoeuf. *The Bogleheads' Guide to Investing*. New York: Wiley, 2006.

Morris, Virginia B., and Kenneth M. Morris. *Standard & Poor's Guide to Money and Investing*. New York: McGraw-Hill, 2005.

O'Neill, William, *How to Make Money in Stocks: A Winning System in Good Times and Bad*. 4th ed. New York: McGraw-Hill, 2009.

Ruffenach, Glenn, and Kelly Greene. *The Wall Street Journal. Complete Retirement Guidebook: How to Plan It, Live It and Enjoy It*. New York: Three Rivers Press, 2007.

When Do I Have to Take Money out of My IRAs?

When I reached my seventieth birthday, my family and friends had a party to help me celebrate. Six months later, when I turned 70½, the only people celebrating were those at the IRS.

As mentioned earlier, the year in which you turn 70½ is when you are required by Uncle Sam to start withdrawing money from your IRAs and most other tax-deferred retirement accounts. (Your Roth IRAs are not included, but assets in Roth 401(k) accounts are, as are inherited Roth IRAs.) And, of course, you have to pay income taxes on some or all of that money. It's no wonder the tax collectors were so happy when I turned 70½. They had waited 20 years for those taxes.

For most of us, paying taxes on IRA withdrawals is a good-news, bad-news story. The good news is that we were wise to save money in tax-deferred retirement accounts for a long time. The bad news is that when it's time to take the money out, most or all of it will be taxable. In my case, this means that for every dollar I take out of my IRAs and spend, I have to take an extra 25 cents out of my non-IRA savings to pay my federal and state taxes.

That hurts, especially if you didn't anticipate that expense when you worked out your retirement budget. Unfortunately, I didn't. But hopefully, if you saved regularly while you were working and invested wisely, you should be able to pay your taxes and have money left over to help pay your living expenses.

However, whether you save a lot of money or a little money in a retirement account, the process of taking the money out—as Uncle Sam requires—will strain your brain. Of course, it helps to know the lingo. In the language used in the IRS regulations, withdrawals from IRAs are called *distributions*. And the whole process of withdrawing money from retirement accounts at 70½ is known as taking your *required minimum distributions* (RMDs).

Thus, if you run into a friend on the street who asks, "Have you taken your RMDs yet?" you can be assured that your friend is not asking whether you've taken your vitamins recently—only whether you've made your IRA withdrawals yet.

Curiously, some mutual funds and financial companies use the phrase "minimum required distributions" (MRDs), while others use "required minimum distributions" (RMDs). Why? Nobody seems to know. But I'm going to go with the IRS version—RMDs. After all, I say, "A tax by any other name is still a tax."

The Rules

Most taxpayers will have to consult only one simple IRS table each year, the Uniform Lifetime Table from IRS publication 590

(Table 6.1), to find the number they need to use to calculate their withdrawals. Most IRA owners will use that table.

There is, however, one exception: if your spouse is the sole beneficiary of your IRA for the entire year and your spouse is also more than 10 years younger than you are, the two of you will use a different IRS table to calculate your withdrawal. It's called the Joint Life and Last Survivor Expectancy Table (Table 6.2).

Although the IRS has simplified the RMD withdrawal process, there are still some aspects that are complicated—especially when they involve beneficiaries. For instance, if you leave your IRA assets to your grandchildren or even your great-grandchildren, this is a likely scenario: if the custodian retains the assets in "an inherited IRA," the custodian, or eventually the young heirs themselves, need withdraw only their basic RMD amounts each year, based on their actuarial life expectancies. That could be 80 years or more (from the IRS Single Life Expectancy Table). That can stretch out the tax-deferred growth potential of much of their inheritance for many years (although they can always withdraw more or actually deplete the account at any time).

But while you are still dealing with your own required withdrawals, be careful to take the right amount. While you are allowed to take out more than the minimum, you'd better not take less, or you could wind up paying a hefty penalty to the IRS: 50 percent of the difference between the amount of money you withdrew and the amount that you should have withdrawn. And then, after paying the penalty, you must still withdraw the correct amount and pay any taxes and interest due on that amount.

I therefore strongly recommend that you consult a financial planner or an accountant before you begin your withdrawals. This is particularly true if you have large sums of money in your retirement plans.

MAKING YOUR FIRST WITHDRAWAL

When it comes to taking your first withdrawal, you have two options. The first is to take your withdrawal in the calendar year in which you become 70½. Or, if you wish, you can wait until April 1 of the following year to take your initial withdrawal and then take a second withdrawal by December 31 of that year.

However, taking two withdrawals in the same year means that you will pay income taxes on two withdrawals instead of one. I elected to take my first withdrawal when I was 70½ because I did not want to pay income taxes on two withdrawals in one year.

If you take your withdrawal in the year in which you turn 70½, you will base it on how much money you had in your retirement accounts as of the previous December 31. As an example, let's say you turn 70½ in 2013. If you take your withdrawal in 2013, it will be based on the amount of money in your accounts on December 31, 2012.

If you want to wait, you must take your first withdrawal by April 1, 2014. If you do that, the withdrawal will still be based on your account total as of December 31, 2012. However, if you do wait, you will then have to take a second withdrawal before December 31, 2014. In this case, the second withdrawal would be based on the amount of money in your accounts as of December 31, 2013.

MAKING A LIST

When you get close to 70½, it's a good time to ask yourself: "How many IRAs or other tax-deferred retirement accounts do I have?" That's an important question because, when you make your withdrawals, you have to consider the assets in all of those accounts. (Roth IRAs are not included.)

Here are some of the tax-deferred accounts that must be considered.

Traditional IRAs

A traditional IRA is a tax-deferred savings account for people who earn income. If you earn income, you also may contribute to a traditional IRA for a nonworking spouse. Contributions to traditional IRAs can be either deductible or nondeductible. A deductible contribution is so named because you were able to take an income tax deduction for the money you put into that account. The amount you put in, together with any earnings on those investments, is taxable when you begin to take money out of that account. A nondeductible contribution is a contribution that you made with after-tax money. You did not receive a tax deduction when you made the contribution. Thus, only the investment earnings portion of each distribution is taxable.

IRA Rollover Accounts

These are accounts that you set up when you roll over money from your 401(k) or a similar retirement plan to an IRA account at a bank, brokerage firm, or mutual fund company.

Simplified Employee Pension Plan (SEP-IRA)

This is a retirement plan for sole proprietors, partners, or corporations. A SEP is set up as an individual employee retirement account, and the employer makes contributions to each separate account.

Savings Incentive Match Plan for Employees (SIMPLE-IRA)

A SIMPLE-IRA is a retirement plan for the self-employed or for a partnership or corporation with up to 100 employees. Employees can make pretax contributions from their pay; employers must make matching or nonmatching contributions.

Defined-Contribution Plans (Including Profit-Sharing and Money Purchase Plans)

In 2013, the most money that could be contributed to a defined-contribution account is $51,000, including both employer and employee contributions. For example, an employee could contribute 100 percent of his salary up to $17,500 (plus an additional catch-up contribution of $5,500 if he was 50 or older). The employer could contribute an additional 25 percent of the employee's salary, with the total not to exceed the overall maximum of $51,000.

Company 401(k) Plan

If an employee who retires leaves money in a company 401(k) plan, she must begin to withdraw money from the retirement account when she reaches 70½ [this includes Roth 401(k) money]. The rules of a particular 401(k) or Roth 401(k) plan may affect how the withdrawals can be made. On the other hand, if you are still working for that employer in the year you reach 70½, and you do not own 5 percent or more of the company, you do not need to begin taking required distributions until April 1 of the calendar year following the year in which you ultimately retire from the company.

403(b) Plan

The 403(b) plan is generally available to employees of tax-exempt organizations such as colleges, universities, hospitals, and charitable groups. Certain mandatory withdrawal rules apply to these plans as well.

DON'T GIVE UP YET

Once you have figured out how many tax-deferred accounts you own, make a list of those accounts and your balances as of the previous December 31. The next step is to find out how much money you must take out of each account in the first year of your RMDs.

To do that, you will have to use one of two IRS life expectancy tables that will show you the divisor to use when you figure out your withdrawals. These two tables are the Uniform Lifetime Table (Table 6.1) and the Joint Life and Last Survivor Expectancy Table (Table 6.2).

The IRS's goal is to make sure that you take out some of your retirement money each year and pay the income taxes due on

TABLE 6.1   Uniform Lifetime Table*

YOUR AGE	YOUR FACTOR	YOUR AGE	YOUR FACTOR
70	27.4	86	14.1
71	26.5	87	13.4
72	25.6	88	12.7
73	24.7	89	12.0
74	23.8	90	11.4
75	22.9	91	10.8
76	22.0	92	10.2
77	21.2	93	9.6
78	20.3	94	9.1
79	19.5	95	8.6
80	18.7	96	8.1
81	17.9	97	7.6
82	17.1	98	7.1
83	16.3	99	6.7
84	15.5	100	6.3
85	14.8		

*For use by owners of IRAs.

Source: Internal Revenue Service.

TABLE 6.2 Joint Life and Last Survivor Expectancy Table*

| | YOUR PRESENT AGE | | | | | | | | | | | | | | | |
SPOUSAL BENEFICIARY AGE	70	71	72	73	74	75	76	77	78	79	80	81	82	83	84	85
50	35.1	35	34.9	34.8	34.8	34.7	34.6	34.6	34.5	34.5	34.5	34.4	34.4	34.4	34.3	34.3
51	34.3	34.2	34.1	34	33.9	33.8	33.8	33.7	33.6	33.6	33.6	33.5	33.5	33.5	33.4	33.4
52	33.4	33.3	33.2	33.1	33	33	32.9	32.8	32.8	32.7	32.7	32.6	32.6	32.6	32.5	32.5
53	32.6	32.5	32.4	32.3	32.2	32.1	32	32	31.9	31.8	31.8	31.8	31.7	31.7	31.7	31.6
54	31.8	31.7	31.6	31.5	31.4	31.3	31.2	31.1	31	31	30.9	30.9	30.8	30.8	30.8	30.7
55	30.3	30.9	30.8	30.6	30.5	30.4	30.3	30.3	30.2	30.1	30.1	30	30	29.9	29.9	29.9
56	29.5	30.1	30	29.8	29.7	29.6	29.5	29.4	29.3	29.3	29.2	29.2	29.1	29.1	29	29
57	28.8	29.4	29.2	29.1	28.9	28.8	28.7	28.6	28.5	28.4	28.4	28.3	28.3	28.2	28.2	28.1
58	28.1	28.6	28.4	28.3	28.1	28	27.9	27.8	27.7	27.6	27.5	27.5	27.4	27.4	27.3	27.3
59		27.9	27.7	27.5	27.4	27.2	27.1	27	26.9	26.8	26.7	26.6	26.6	26.5	26.5	26.4
60		27.2	27	26.8	26.6	26.5	26.3	26.2	26.1	26	25.9	25.8	25.8	25.7	25.6	25.6
61			26.3	26.1	25.9	25.7	25.6	25.4	25.3	25.2	25.1	25	24.9	24.9	24.8	24.8
62				25.4	25.2	25	24.8	24.7	24.6	24.4	24.3	24.2	24.1	24.1	24	23.9

63	24.5	24.3	24.1	23.9	23.8	23.7	23.6	23.4	23.4	23.3	23.2	23.1
64		23.6	23.4	23.2	23.1	22.9	22.8	22.7	22.6	22.5	22.4	22.3
65			22.7	22.5	22.4	22.2	22.1	21.9	21.8	21.7	21.6	21.6
66				21.8	21.7	21.5	21.3	21.2	21.1	21	20.9	20.8
67					21	20.8	20.6	20.5	20.4	20.2	20.1	20.1
68						20.1	20	19.8	19.7	19.5	19.4	19.3
69							19.3	19.1	19	18.8	18.7	18.6
70								18.5	18.3	18.2	18	17.9
71									17.7	17.5	17.4	17.3
72										16.9	16.7	16.6
73											16.1	16
74												15.4

* Use this table to determine your life expectancy factor only if your sole primary beneficiary is a spouse who is more than 10 years younger than you are. To determine your 2013 RMD, divide your year-end retirement account balance as of December 31, 2012, by the divisor in the table above that corresponds to your age and your spouse's age as of December 31, 2013. For example, if you will be age 73 as of December 31, 2013, and your spouse will be age 62 as of that date, the life expectancy factor used to calculate your 2013 RMD would be 25.4.

Source: T. Rowe Price.

that money. If you die before the end of your withdrawal period, your beneficiary may have the option to continue withdrawing annual payments from the account beginning in the year following your death. Note that your beneficiary, like you, can always take more, but never less, than the minimum required amount each year. Otherwise, penalties will apply.

When a husband dies, his widow-beneficiary can roll over the IRA into her own IRA, and once she attains age 70½, she can use the favorable Uniform Lifetime Table (Table 6.1) to calculate her RMDs.

To use Table 6.1, locate your age. The number next to your age will be the divisor. If you are using Table 6.2, use your age and the age of your beneficiary to locate your divisor.

To calculate your withdrawals, divide the amount of money in each of your retirement accounts by your divisor. That's where your list will come in handy. The IRS says that you must do the calculation for each of your retirement accounts.

For IRAs and 403(b) accounts, here's how it works: if you own four deductible IRAs or four 403(b) accounts, each with a balance of $20,000 as of December 31, 2011, and your withdrawal factor for the first year is 27.4, you will have to withdraw a minimum of $730 from each of the four accounts, or a total of $2,920. You may take the money out of one IRA account or more than one IRA account. Similarly, if you have 403(b) accounts, you may take all the money out of those accounts. You may not combine 403(b) and IRA balances, however.

Now, let's assume that you have a fifth IRA. In this case, you contributed $10,000 in *after-tax* dollars to this account (unlike the other four IRAs). Over the years, it gained another $10,000, for a total of $20,000. Under IRS rules, the $10,000 you contributed after tax is not taxable.

So what do you do? Under this scenario, according to financial planner Christine S. Fahlund at T. Rowe Price Investment

Services, you must total up the value of all your IRA accounts or the value of all your 403(b) accounts. In this case, the total is $100,000 (five accounts of $20,000 each). Then you have to figure out what portion of your withdrawals is not taxable.

Here's how the arithmetic goes: of the $100,000 in your accounts, $10,000, or 10 percent, was contributed in after-tax money. We already know that you have to withdraw $730 from each account, for a total of $3,650 (five accounts multiplied by $730). However, only 90 percent of that amount is taxable.

For each of the $730 withdrawals, you would have to pay taxes on only $657. Thus, for the five accounts, the total taxable amount of the withdrawals would be $3,285 (five accounts multiplied by $657). The other $365 comes out tax-free.

When I made my first IRA withdrawal, I tried to be careful to take the right amount so that I would not be penalized for taking out less than required. You, too, should be careful.

How to Use the Life-Expectancy Tables

As I noted, the IRS gives you two tables to help you figure out your withdrawals. The IRS also provides a third table that is intended for use by your beneficiaries after your death.

Here is a rundown on how all three of these tables in IRS publication 590 are to be used (using a $100,000 IRA as an example).

Table 6.1 is the Uniform Lifetime Table. It is the table that will be used by most individuals who must withdraw money from their IRAs and other tax-deferred accounts.

At age 70½, assuming that your seventieth birthday was in the current calendar year, your divisor would be 27.4. Divide $100,000 by 27.4, and you get $3,650, the amount of your initial minimum withdrawal. In the following year, when you celebrate your seventy-first birthday, you return to the Uniform Lifetime

Table, select the new divisor, 26.5, and divide that figure into your new December 31 balance to obtain the amount of your RMD in Year 2.

Table 6.2 is the Joint Life and Last Survivor Expectancy Table. This should be used in cases where your spouse is the sole beneficiary of your account and is more than 10 years younger than you are.

For instance, if you are 73 and your spouse is 62—11 years younger—the table shows that your divisor is 25.4. If your account is worth $100,000, your first-year minimum withdrawal would be $100,000 divided by 25.4, or $3,937. Each year thereafter, the two of you go back to the Joint Life and Last Survivor Expectancy Table, find your new divisor, and divide that factor into your new December 31 balance. After the first spouse dies, the surviving spouse rolls over the IRA to her own name, then takes RMDs in future years using a factor based solely on her own age found in the Uniform Lifetime Table.

Table 6.3, the Single Life Expectancy Table, is used mostly by nonspouse beneficiaries. Let's say that John, 74, dies when his daughter, Mary, is 41. Mary is John's beneficiary on his IRA account. In the year following John's death, Mary, who is now 42, consults the table and finds that, based on her current age, her divisor is 41.7, meaning that she can take withdrawals from John's IRA account for more than 40 years. If the account balance was $100,000 on December 31 of the year of John's death, Mary's first minimum withdrawal would be $2,398 ($100,000 divided by 41.7). She can always take more than the RMD amount in any given year. In the second year, Mary does not need to go back to the Single Life Expectancy Table. Instead, she subtracts one year from her RMD factor, or divisor, of 41.7 to arrive at her new factor of 40.7 and divides her new December 31 ending balance by that factor. The following year, her factor would be 39.7, and so forth.

TABLE 6.3 Single Life Expectancy Table*

AGE	LIFE EXPECTANCY	AGE	LIFE EXPECTANCY	AGE	LIFE EXPECTANCY
0	82.4	30	53.3	60	25.2
1	81.6	31	52.4	61	24.4
2	80.6	32	51.4	62	23.5
3	79.7	33	50.4	63	22.7
4	78.7	34	49.4	64	21.8
5	77.7	35	48.5	65	21.0
6	76.7	36	47.5	66	20.2
7	75.8	37	46.5	67	19.4
8	74.8	38	45.6	68	18.6
9	73.8	39	44.6	69	17.8
10	72.8	40	43.6	70	17.0
11	71.8	41	42.7	71	16.3
12	70.8	42	41.7	72	15.5
13	69.9	43	40.7	73	14.8
14	68.9	44	39.8	74	14.1
15	67.9	45	38.8	75	13.4
16	66.9	46	37.9	76	12.7
17	66.0	47	37.0	77	12.1
18	65.0	48	36.0	78	11.4
19	64.0	49	35.1	79	10.8
20	63.0	50	34.2	80	10.2
21	62.1	51	33.3	81	9.7
22	61.1	52	32.3	82	9.1
23	60.1	53	31.4	83	8.6
24	59.1	54	30.5	84	8.1
25	58.2	55	29.6	85	7.6
26	57.2	56	28.7	86	7.1
27	56.2	57	27.9	87	6.7
28	55.3	58	27.0	88	6.3
29	54.3	59	26.1	89	5.9

(continued on next page)

TABLE 6.3 Single Life Expectancy Table* (continued)

AGE	LIFE EXPECTANCY	AGE	LIFE EXPECTANCY	AGE	LIFE EXPECTANCY
90	5.5	98	3.4	106	1.7
91	5.2	99	3.1	107	1.5
92	4.9	100	2.9	108	1.4
93	4.6	101	2.7	109	1.2
94	4.3	102	2.5	110	1.1
95	4.1	103	2.3	111+	1.0
96	3.8	104	2.1		
97	3.6	105	1.9		

*For use by beneficiaries.

Source: Internal Revenue Service.

Summing Up

Well, those are the bare bones of the process for taking IRA withdrawals. If you are embarking on this process, I suggest that you start early, study your options carefully, and get all the advice you can find. You'll get through it. Then, along with me, you will wonder: why is retirement such hard work?

For More Information

The IRS life-expectancy tables are contained in IRS publication 590, *Individual Retirement Arrangements (IRAs)*. To order the booklet, call 1-800-829-3676. You can also download the publication from the IRS website: www.irs.gov.

Vanguard offers an RMD (required minimum distribution) kit that is available on its website, www.vanguard.com (under forms), or by calling Vanguard Retail Services, 1-800-662-7447.

The T. Rowe Price website has a section devoted to the topic of RMDs, with tools to help you estimate the amount you may need to withdraw and to set up an automated RMD program for IRAs held at T. Rowe Price. You can find this information at www.troweprice.com/rmd.

T. Rowe Price also publishes the *T. Rowe Price Guide for IRA and 403(b) Account Beneficiaries*. It explains the options available to beneficiaries who inherit these accounts. It can be downloaded from the website mentioned earlier (www.troweprice.com/rmd).

How Should I Invest During Retirement?

Three years after I retired, I was shocked to discover that if my wife and I didn't cut down on our spending and get better results on our investments, we would use up all our retirement savings within eight years. As you can imagine, that was extremely bad news, because at that point, I was only 72 and my wife, Sara, was 70. In eight years, I would be only 80 and Sara would be 78—not terribly old by today's standards. In fact, Sara and I have many friends who are 80 or older and still lead active, interesting lives.

The truth of the matter is, I was hoping that our savings would last until we were in our nineties. But my calculations told me that we would fall far short of that goal.

Now, I'm not suggesting that if we used up our savings, we would be penniless. Sara and I are fortunate in having regular retirement incomes. Together with our Social Security benefits, our pension checks help pay for our basic living expenses. However, we were using our savings to take occasional vacation trips and to otherwise enjoy our retirement. Without any savings to draw upon, our activities would have been very limited.

How did I discover that our savings were dwindling rapidly? By using one of those "retirement calculators" that are so popular on the Internet. I went online to the website operated by Vanguard mutual funds, www.vanguard.com. I located the company's retirement planning page and found a program that calculates how long your retirement savings will last. (The Vanguard computer program is one of several such programs available from financial service companies. A list is included at the end of the chapter.)

I then entered my financial information, responding to the questions that appeared on my screen. When I was finished, I clicked on the "calculate" button, and the machine went to work. It digested my numbers and quickly rendered its verdict. It told me that I would use up all my savings by 2007. That was only eight years away.

The cause of the problem soon became apparent: we were dipping into our savings too often and not earning enough on our investments to replace the money that we were taking out. And, of course, the more our nest egg shrank, the less it earned. Although I didn't like what the computer was telling me, I was grateful to get the warning in time to do something about it.

The first thing I did was to look at some "what-if" calculations. I tried several different scenarios to see what I could do to make our savings last longer. I lowered our monthly expenses and raised the earnings on our investments. That seemed to help. The revised numbers had the effect of stretching out our savings for a few additional years.

But then I realized that I had told the computer that I would continue to work as a freelance writer until I was 90. On reflection, that seemed to be a bit of a stretch, so I went back and told the computer that I would stop earning additional income at age 80. That made the picture worse.

The calculations left me with little choice but to think seriously about how much money Sara and I could save if we trimmed our living expenses. If that was what we had to do, I'd do it. But, frankly, it was not a happy prospect.

Making Ends Meet

To get a fresh perspective on my problem, I chatted with Duane Cabrera, a principal at Vanguard. Cabrera's main goal was to educate retirees and help them to manage their finances successfully throughout retirement.

"There is no magic bullet to keep from running out of money," Cabrera said. "At the end of the day, a retiree's success will be driven by his or her ability to maximize income and minimize expenses."

Cabrera said he has often observed that "retirees have a tendency to understate their expenses and overstate their income." Then, when they are faced with higher-than-expected expenses, they draw out more money from their accounts than is wise. One key to financial success during retirement is to use realistic assumptions about expenses, income, and investment returns when preparing a retirement plan.

Cabrera believes that when people first retire, they should not take out more than 3 to 4 percent of their savings each year. When they get into their seventies, he said, they may be able to increase their withdrawals to 4 to 5 percent. But the key to financial success in retirement is keeping control of one's expenses.

In any event, it seems clear that retirees cannot assume, as many have done in the past, that they will consistently earn 6 to 7 percent on their money. As we saw during 2008 and 2009, a stock market that can rise 20 percent in good years can also fall 30 or 40 percent or more in bad years. Thus, retirees should be prepared to adjust their withdrawals based on market conditions in order to ensure that they are not withdrawing too much from their portfolios.

Making Your Savings Last

I wish now that I had run my finances through the Vanguard calculator long before I retired. I would have had a much more realistic idea of how much money we would need to pay our expenses through a 15- to 20-year retirement. I also would have tried harder to improve the returns on our investments.

Until you retire, I discovered, you don't think much about the difference between managing your money in retirement and managing it while you're working. When you're working—and saving for retirement—you pay your bills from your salary or wages, and you try your best to let your savings sit there and grow. But when you retire and you lose your regular paycheck, you are dependent on Social Security, pension checks (if you have a pension), and income from savings. You may also need to work part-time to help out.

If you have maximized your income and minimized your expenses, but you still face a gap between what's coming in and what's going out, you will have to see whether it is possible for you to earn more from your investments. You will have to think carefully about the money in your retirement savings accounts: how that money is invested, what it earns, and how much you can reasonably withdraw each year without seriously reducing the earnings potential of your nest egg. Table 7.1 shows you how long your money will last, depending on the percent you earn each year and the percent you withdraw each year.

TABLE 7.1 When Will Your Savings Run Out?

Savings Growth Rate	2%	3%	4%	5%	6%	7%	8%	9%	10%	11%	12%	13%	14%	15%	16%
15%															20
14%														21	16
13%													22	16	14
12%												23	17	14	12
11%											24	18	15	13	11
10%										25	19	15	13	12	10
9%									27	20	16	14	12	11	10
8%								29	21	17	14	12	11	10	9
7%							31	22	18	15	13	11	10	9	9
6%						33	24	19	16	14	12	11	10	9	8
5%					37	26	20	17	14	12	11	10	9	8	8
4%				41	28	22	18	15	13	12	10	9	9	8	7
3%			47	31	23	19	16	14	12	11	10	9	8	8	7
2%		55	35	26	20	17	15	13	11	10	9	8	8	7	7
1%	70	41	29	22	18	15	13	12	11	10	9	8	7	7	6
	2%	3%	4%	5%	6%	7%	8%	9%	10%	11%	12%	13%	14%	15%	16%

Withdrawal Rate

Source: Oppenheimer Funds, Inc. This chart is intended as educational material about savings and investing and does not predict or depict the rate of return on any mutual fund or other investment. Consult an investment professional for a more specific and detailed analysis of your personal financial situation.

Determine the number of years that your money will last by picking your savings growth rate and your rate of withdrawal. (The chart assumes that you are not adding to your savings.) The number at the intersection of these two rates is how many years may be left before your savings are depleted. For example, if your savings grow 3 percent annually and you withdraw your original principal at a rate of 10 percent annually, your savings may last roughly 12 years.

There are three main ways to invest your retirement savings: you can invest for growth, for income, or for a combination of growth and income. This chapter offers some suggestions on how to use your savings to provide a flow of monthly income and some growth as well.

Investing is a highly personal matter involving your financial needs, your time horizon, and your willingness to take risk. That being the case, I believe it's wise for each investor to discuss her goals with a financial planner or investment advisor. If you are already retired, an advisor can help you figure out how long your money will last in retirement. If you are still working, an advisor can help you develop an investment plan that will help you reach your goals. Suggestions on how to find a financial planner appear at the end of the chapter.

In the meantime, I am happy to share with you some of the lessons I have learned from my years of investing, watching the market, and making investment mistakes. If you expect to depend on your savings to help support you in retirement, these are lessons that you, too, will need to learn. So here they are.

FIVE GOLDEN RULES

You Must Learn How to Invest
If you are still working and you are enrolled in a 401(k) or some other company savings plan, you are probably making decisions

regarding how to invest your money by choosing from among a small number of investments offered by your company. If you are retired, you still have to make investment choices, but now you can choose from 8,000 mutual funds, at least 8,000 stocks, more than 700 exchange-traded funds (ETFs), and countless bonds. And that can be mind-boggling.

In either case, if you haven't already done so, it is time for you to learn how to invest. It is pretty obvious that knowing how to invest is now a required life skill in American society. The ability to save and invest wisely could enable millions of retirees to have a decent lifestyle while they are living into their eighties and beyond. I can foresee the day when the four educational basics will be reading, writing, arithmetic—and investing.

Learning to invest is not difficult. Start with some of the popular investment magazines and TV channels that cover the financial markets on a daily basis. Take a look at some of the many investment websites. There are dozens of books and videos that offer insights into investing. Remember this: before you invest your money, invest your time and learn the basics of investing. It's not hard, and it can even be fun. But start now. You owe it to yourself.

The Greater the Risk, the Greater the Reward

As surely as day follows night, the one rule that never changes on Wall Street is that risk and reward go hand in hand. The greater the risk, the greater the reward, and the greater the reward, the greater the risk. It sounds like a warning you might have gotten from a social studies teacher in high school, but anybody who has been burned in the financial markets knows that this old rule is true. You simply can't get huge gains without taking huge risks. And what goes up very fast can also come down very fast, as we learned from two market events in recent memory: the collapse of high-flying Internet stocks during the spring of 2000 and the once-in-a-century stock market crash in 2008–2009, which was caused by a meltdown in the subprime mortgage, banking, and housing sectors. So, when you make any investment, always think about your tolerance for risk versus your desire for safety.

Never Try to Outguess the Market

Those of us who have been investing for a number of years know the truth of this statement. Remember, in Decision 5, my tale of losing $70,000 in my 401(k) plan? As I discovered, if you sell everything and get out of the market because you think it is going down, chances are that you will sell at the lowest point and be out of the market when it rebounds. Thus, you will get the losses and miss the gains. Experienced investors know that over the last 112 years, the long-term trend of the market has been up, and that if you ignored the short-term gyrations and stayed invested, you would have benefited from those upward movements. Understandably, the financial tsunami in 2008 and 2009 was so traumatic that many investors found it difficult to restrain themselves from selling. But, true to form, after stock prices hit bottom in March 2009, they rebounded strongly in the following months.

Go for the Averages

One of the most tantalizing rules of investing is, "Buy low and sell high." It sounds easy, but it's a very hard thing to do on a consistent basis, as experienced traders will tell you. For investors like you and me, the next best thing is something called *dollar cost averaging*. This involves investing the same amount of money in, say, a mutual fund every month over a long period of time. As the price of the fund's shares rises and falls, you will sometimes buy at the highs and sometimes at the lows. But in the long run, you will be buying your shares at an average price, which is a good deal. In any event, it certainly beats trying to decide when it is the right time to buy those shares, since you are likely to guess wrong.

Spread Your Risk

As kids, we learned the old rule, "Don't put all your eggs in one basket." Why? Because if you drop your basket, good-bye eggs. Thus, it makes sense to put your eggs in more than one basket.

That rule has turned out to be good advice for investors, too. People on Wall Street have their own word for it. They call it *diversification*. Decades of experience have shown that your best chance to succeed as an investor is to put portions of your money into several different kinds of investments.

Specifically, diversification involves putting some of your money in stocks, some in bonds, and some in money market funds. Within each category, you also have a number of choices. For instance, you can invest in stocks of big companies or stocks of small companies, stocks of domestic firms or stocks of foreign firms. With regard to bonds, you can choose among government bonds, corporate bonds, municipal bonds, and others. Money market funds vary in their interest rates, but they are basically similar to one another.

The principle of diversification rests on the fact that different types of investments march to the beats of different drummers. When stocks are going up, bonds may be going down, or vice versa. Similarly, when domestic stocks are rising, foreign stocks may be falling. In short, different investments behave differently at different times and, of course, give you different results. By spreading your money around, you can reduce your chances of being hurt financially if one sector of the market takes a big hit. Of course, all of that is true under what I would consider "normal" market conditions. During the vast sell-off of 2008–2009, market conditions were anything but normal. In fact, it was one of the few times in market history when diversification did not work because almost everything went down. There was simply no place to hide. So, even though diversification has a good long-term track record, it is not infallible.

Meanwhile, here's another note of caution about diversification: some investors try to diversify by buying shares in many mutual funds. That may work if the funds have been carefully selected to represent different areas of the investment world, such as large companies, small companies, domestic companies, international companies, and so on. But all too often, investors unknowingly buy several funds that all specialize in, say, large-cap value stocks. While the funds' names are different, their investment philosophies are the same. Thus, instead of getting diversification, the investor gets a similar result from each of the funds—and more risk than anticipated.

BEYOND THE GOLDEN RULES

Once you are comfortable with the idea of diversification, you will want to think about what portions of your money you want to put into stocks, bonds, and money market funds. Here again, Wall Street has an apt phrase. It's called *asset allocation*.

Slicing the Investment Pie

There are many ways to slice your investment pie. You can cut it in three pieces—one for stocks, one for bonds, and one for money market funds. You can cut it in half and put 50 percent in stocks and 50 percent in bonds. Or you can put 50 percent in stocks, 40 percent in bonds, and 10 percent in money market funds. You get the idea.

But why does it matter how you allocate your money? Earlier, we talked about diversification and how spreading your money around in different investments was your best protection against the short-term ups and downs of the market. Now, let's look at asset allocation. By my definition, that's a strategy that advises us to lean in the same direction as the market. If stocks appear to be in an uptrend, let's switch some of our bond money to stocks. Instead of being 50–50 in stocks and bonds, we'll be 80 percent in stocks and 20 percent in bonds.

Professional investors spend a lot of time trying to decide how to allocate their money. If they judge the direction of stocks or bonds correctly, they will do well. And so can you. Becoming an informed investor will help you develop a sense of how the financial markets are moving. And that can help you make intelligent and profitable investment decisions.

Retirees—a Special Case

For many years, the common wisdom in the investment world was that stocks were suitable for younger investors, but not for older investors. The theory was that once you reached retirement age, you should become more conservative and move your money into bonds and other fixed-income investments, which were judged to be less risky. The thinking was that retirees had to be wary of investing in stocks because, in the event of a market crash, they would lose the savings they needed to live on and might not have time to wait for the market to return to higher ground.

During the decades of the 1980s and 1990s, that view of retirement investing was replaced by another view, which holds that retirees should not give up their stocks and move all their money into bonds when they turn 65. In fact, despite the events of 2008–2009, it's still believed that it makes perfect sense for retirees to keep a significant percentage of their money in equities. And here is why.

The Longevity Case

The Census Bureau tells us that the average 65-year-old can look forward to at least 15 years or more in retirement. Many retirees live into their eighties and even nineties. This is a huge change in life expectancy for most Americans. In 1900, an average 65-year-old had a life expectancy of only a few years. Currently, an average 65-year-old man can expect to live to about age 81. Women can expect to reach about age 84.

If today's retirees have that many years to invest, why shouldn't they take advantage of the higher returns they can get from stocks? The historical record is persuasive: over the 86 years from 1926 through 2011, large-company stocks returned an average of 9.8 percent a year, while long-term government bonds returned 5.7 percent a year, according to Ibbotson Associates, a subsidiary of Morningstar, Inc. By investing in stocks, it would appear, retirees can improve their chances of stretching out their retirement dollars. But be cautious. The long upward climb in the Ibbotson stock market chart obscures the many market crashes and financial upheavals that have taken their toll on all investors—but especially on people who are preparing to retire.

Inflation Is Not Your Friend

Our new and longer investment horizons mean that retirees have to worry more about inflation than they did before. Inflation has always been a concern for individuals who live on fixed incomes, but before the dramatic increase in life expectancy, there may have been less concern about the effects of inflation on retirees. After all, if your retirement was going to last for only a few years, you didn't have to worry much about inflation. But if your retirement is going to last for 15 or 20 years, inflation can have a substantial impact on the value of your savings.

Although inflation has been subdued in recent years, it averaged 2.86 percent a year during the 26 years from 1985 through 2011, according to the folks at T. Rowe Price. For example, if you retired at the beginning of 1985 with $20,000 in savings, the impact of inflation would have reduced your purchasing power to $9,334 by the end of 2011. That's why today's retirees are advised not to be too conservative in their investments. It may seem safe to put all of one's savings in money market funds, bank CDs, or even government bonds, but without long-term growth in your portfolio, your savings can be zapped by inflation.

Your goal as a retiree should be to develop an investment portfolio that provides relative safety, current income for living expenses, and growth of your savings. How can you do this? The best way is to use a mix of stock, bond, and money market instruments, tailored to your special situation and needs. While stocks suffer from more ups and downs than bonds do, you can reduce the volatility of your stock investments by using conservative mutual funds such as equity income funds, which invest in high-yielding stocks, and balanced funds, which invest in a mix of stocks and bonds. Research by T. Rowe Price shows that in falling markets, these types of funds declined less and came back faster than the overall market.

Our Changing Financial Markets

Financial markets have changed dramatically in the last several decades. Some of these developments have been good for individual investors; others have not. The changes include:

- *The creation of the 401(k) plan.* These plans have allowed millions of Americans to save and invest for retirement at the places where they work. This, in turn, has created several generations of new investors whose financial futures depend on the ups and downs of the stock and bond markets.

- *The rise of the mutual fund industry.* The industry grew during the 1980s and 1990s. Today, there are more than 8,600 mutual funds holding trillions of dollars belonging to millions of people who are saving not only for retirement, but to buy a house or send their kids to college. The investment companies have created a broad menu of funds that allow individuals to invest across a wide range of industries and countries.

- *The emergence of "financial engineering."* Now a dominant factor on Wall Street, financial engineering created the ill-fated subprime mortgage derivatives that destroyed banks, brokerages, and mortgage companies and cost the nation billions of dollars in bailouts. Meanwhile, Wall Street's wizards have developed advanced electronic strategies that enable them to "flash" trade millions of shares of stock in a second. While this may be good for the professionals, it makes me wonder whether it is futile for me, as an individual investor, to compete in the market against these electronic powerhouses.

- *The sleaze on Wall Street.* The financial markets have always had their share of scandals and illegal behavior. But the multiple outrages of the last 20 years—from the investment bank abuses of the Ponzi scheme of Bernard Madoff—seem to have marked a new high in bad behavior and a new low in investor confidence in Wall Street and its regulators. For many investors, it may be a long time before they feel they can put their trust in the investment markets.

Turning Your Nest Egg into Income

Many retirees, I have found, need to use their savings to produce a monthly income that can help them close the gap between their income and their monthly living expenses. The question is, what's the best way to accomplish this goal? I took the question to a friend, Jack R. May, a Certified Financial Planner (CFP) at the firm of Lara, Shull, & May, LLC, in Falls Church, Virginia. I met Jack 25 years ago when I wanted to develop a better understanding of financial markets, investments, and corporate accounting. At the time, he was teaching financial planning at George Washington University in Washington, DC. I enrolled in a couple of his courses and learned many valuable things.

I asked Jack what he would recommend to a person who retires at age 66 with Social Security benefits, a company pension, and $100,000 accumulated over many years in a company 401(k) plan. In this scenario, the retiree has rolled over his money into a tax-deferred IRA account at a brokerage firm or a mutual fund company. The retiree's basic goal would be twofold: to get as much income as possible and to preserve his nest egg as long as possible by taking only investment income from the $100,000, leaving the principal intact.

One small wrinkle is that at age 70½, as described in Decision 6, retirees must begin to take money out of their tax-deferred retirement accounts. Of course, there is nothing to prevent a retiree from reinvesting that money in a taxable account. At 70½, the required minimum distribution (RMD) formula requires a roughly 3.65 percent withdrawal to start with, but the RMD increases to nearly 5 percent by age 78.

One other wrinkle is that many studies have shown that the best way for retirees to make their savings last through retirement is to withdraw no more than 5 percent a year—in this case, $5,000. To that, we would add an annual inflation adjustment of 3 percent of the 5 percent, or $150. Although current year-over-year inflation was just 1.7 percent as of July 31, 2012, the long-term average is closer to 3 percent.

So I asked Jack, what would be the best way for a 66-year-old retiree to invest $100,000 to produce a steady flow of monthly income? Also, what risks would be associated with these investment strategies?

I have asked Jack these questions in the past. But in the fall of 2012, as the fourth edition was being written, Jack's search for income-producing investments had become far more difficult because of the historically low interest-rate environment created by the Federal Reserve to cope with the slow recovery from the 2008–2009 recession. Ben Bernanke, chairman of the Federal Reserve, recently stated that he intends to hold short-term rates low (now between 0 percent and 0.25 percent) through 2014. Currently, in the fall of 2012, Jack is looking at yields for three-month Treasury bills and money market accounts that are at or near zero percent. Rates for CDs are only slightly higher. Jack said he found that "a laddered CD/Treasury bond strategy would generate only an annual yield of just over 1.25 percent." Thus, except for the most conservative retiree who can afford these exceptionally low rates, he is not suggesting a CD or Treasury strategy, as the yields are simply too low now and into the foreseeable future.

Nevertheless, Jack accepted the challenge and suggested five different investment choices:

1. A multisector bond mutual fund

2. A high-quality dividend-paying stock portfolio

3. A variable annuity

4. A managed diversified portfolio strategy

5. A managed portfolio of exchange-traded funds

In addition, Jack said that before retirees decide where to invest, they must decide how much income they need to generate from their investments. If their portfolios produce more than 5 percent in a given year, they should leave the remainder invested to help their savings grow.

"Another important objective," Jack said, "is not just to provide a required income and preserve your principal today, but to keep pace with inflation tomorrow." At just 3 percent inflation, he noted, prices will double in 24 years. Although the 2000–2002 and 2008–2009 market crashes have left many people wary of stocks, Jack said that the best long-run returns have come from stocks. U.S. stocks, he said, offer ownership positions in some of the best companies in the world. Jack thus believes that retirees should keep at least a portion of their savings in dividend-paying stocks or dividend-paying mutual funds.

Something else that retirees should know before retiring and deciding on a strategy, Jack said, is what he calls "the math of loss." Prior to retirement, many investors accumulated money by means of dollar cost averaging. This is the method of investing periodically, such as monthly, to take advantage of the ups and downs of the market.

With that strategy, when prices dropped, the investor picked up more shares, and when prices rose, the portfolio was more valuable. Jack said, "While accumulating your nest egg, you might think that volatility was your friend. However, that is *not* so during retirement."

Let's assume, Jack said, that an investor had a $100,000 portfolio in the stock market and it dropped by 50 percent (almost exactly what happened from September 2008 to March 2009). Further assume that a 5 percent income distribution, or $5,000, is being withdrawn from the $100,000 at the beginning of the year. After this drop, what rate of return does the investor need for her portfolio to get back to $100,000? Jack describes it this way. "The quick answer is, if you lose 50 percent, you would need a 50 percent rebound to break even. But that is simply not the case! A 50 percent return brings the portfolio back to just $75,000.

Instead, a $50,000 portfolio would need to double in value. In other words, it would need a 100 percent increase to break even. But the worst part is this: consider that the $5,000 income is now being withdrawn from a $50,000 portfolio—no longer a 5 percent distribution but a 10 percent distribution. This becomes a much more difficult portfolio to sustain over time."

The idea of the math of loss leads to a concept referred to as the "sequence of returns." It means that it matters when an individual retires. Two portfolios with exactly the same average annual returns over time may end with dramatically different results based on when the "good years" and the "bad years" occurred. Individuals who retire and begin to withdraw income just prior to a downturn in their portfolios may have a difficult time recovering even if they have good returns thereafter, compared with a retiree whose portfolio has positive returns when he starts withdrawing from it. This is true even if both portfolios have the exact same average annual returns over time!

Thus, new retirees must be cautious about the timing and amount of their withdrawals. They also should seek investments with lower volatility. Remember, one of the fastest-growing segments of the population is people turning 100 years old. Here are Jack May's five choices for a $100,000 investment that produce income.

MULTISECTOR BOND MUTUAL FUND

Bonds are loans, typically made by investors to governments or corporations. Investors receive interest payments, usually every six months, and get their original principal back upon maturity. Mutual fund managers often buy and sell bonds and will have bonds with different interest rates and maturities in their funds. A fund's rate, then, is a blend of the rates on all the bonds in the portfolio.

When bonds are sold initially, they are given credit ratings that reflect the financial soundness of the government agency or business that issues them. The highest rating is AAA. Any bond rated between AAA and BBB is considered an investment-grade bond. Anything below BBB is often referred to as a "junk bond."

The global bond market is enormous and complex, much larger than the global stock market. Bonds are issued by governments, municipalities, and corporations and can vary widely in credit quality, time to maturity, and other criteria. More important, unlike the situation with stocks, where it is easy to find the exact price and there are indexes such as the Dow Jones Industrial Average or the Standard & Poor's 500 that indicate how the market overall is doing, bond prices are not that easy to find. In many cases, bond prices are not even fixed, but negotiated.

Until recent years, most sovereign (government) bonds were of the highest quality. However, this began to change when European countries began to experience economic problems. In the case of Greece, in the spring of 2012, the country had essentially defaulted on roughly 74 percent of its government and foreign-law bonds, according to Fitch Ratings. In the United States, mounting federal debt loads prompted a Standard & Poor's credit downgrade in the summer of 2011. There are now more AAA corporate bonds than AAA sovereign bonds. Not surprisingly, companies with lower credit ratings pay a higher interest rate on their bonds than do companies with higher credit ratings. Those higher interest payments are what make junk bonds so attractive to investors. However, investors in high-yield bonds face the "business risk" that a company might not be able to pay the interest on its bonds. The advantage of using mutual funds is that fund managers have analysts who review the bonds before the fund purchases them. Also, the fund managers can get better prices for bonds than individuals can get on their own, partly as a result of buying in volume. In addition, most bond funds pay out on a monthly basis and thus are ideal for providing retirement income.

All bond funds are subject to certain risks, especially the movement of interest rates. When interest rates rise, the value of a bond will decline—and vice versa. In the summer of 2012, because of an ongoing flight to quality resulting from uncertainty around the euro, government bonds rose in price and many were selling at premiums to face value, thus producing historically low yields. The 10-year Treasury bond dropped to a yield of 1.42 percent.

The primary goal of many bond funds is to produce income. There are a wide variety of different bond funds available to the investor. They can be categorized generally by risk, from lower to higher based on the quality and types of bonds in the portfolio. While some managers may specifically buy Treasury bonds, others may buy corporate or international bonds. Still others buy a diverse portfolio of bonds to either protect the investor against loss or increase the yield (or both). Funds of these latter types usually have "strategic" or "diversified" in their names. A few of the many mutual fund companies with these diversified funds include Fidelity, Franklin, and John Hancock Strategic Income funds.

If interest rates were to rise, bond prices would fall, but Treasury and corporate bonds often move in different directions, so the diversity of these funds would help cushion any loss. Also, if interest rates were to rise over time, the fund managers would be able to add higher-yielding bonds to the portfolio as new money is invested in their fund.

Before investing in any mutual funds or annuities, it is important to read through the prospectus carefully. There you will find information about expenses, the fund's holdings, and its philosophy, as well as its risks and how it is run.

HIGH-QUALITY DIVIDEND-PAYING STOCK PORTFOLIO

When a company earns a profit, it has several choices for how best to deploy those funds. It can offer bonuses to its employees, contribute extra to the corporate retirement plan, or reinvest in its business. In addition, it can pay a dividend to its shareholders. When a company starts paying a dividend, it is usually a long-term commitment. Thus, paying a dividend is a big decision and one that only companies with strong balance sheets and good earnings are likely to make.

Typically, then, an investor who is buying a portfolio of dividend-paying stocks owns stocks in large, high-quality companies, such as Exxon Mobil, McDonald's, and Coca-Cola. In addition, many companies increase their dividends as their profits increase. This is very different from buying most bonds, which have a fixed payout (coupon) for the life of the bond. Increasing dividends may also help offset the effects of inflation.

Another reason to consider a dividend-paying stock portfolio at this time is that some companies may pay a dividend that is actually higher than their bond interest. This is very unusual, however. Many mutual fund companies manage portfolios of this type, usually with "equity income" or "dividend" in their names.

Some examples of these funds include Vanguard Equity Income, BlackRock Equity Dividend, Franklin Rising Dividends Fund, and American Funds' Washington Mutual Investors Fund, one of the oldest funds. Even these funds are managed differently, as some look more for higher dividend yields now and likely lower total returns later, while others buy lower yields now with the expectation that the companies will increase their dividends more quickly into the future. The yields on these funds currently vary from 1 or 2 percent to 4 or 5 percent, depending on the manager.

VARIABLE ANNUITY

Annuities are designed by insurance companies to allow an individual to accumulate a nest egg for retirement, which then can be used to provide a reliable income.

There are two main types of annuities—fixed and variable. Both offer the investor a guaranteed lifetime income, but in quite different ways. Both fixed and variable annuities (with appropriate additional options) remove the adverse consequences associated with the sequence of returns and the math of loss. Both of these concepts are concerned with withdrawing money from a portfolio while it is dropping in value, which increases the chance of running out of money. Annuities with appropriate features will pay a steady income throughout the lives of both spouses, even if the underlying portfolio drops to $0.

A fixed annuity typically converts your investment into a guaranteed income for life. This often provides a high payout because your return comes from both principal and interest. A positive aspect of fixed annuities is that the principal portion of the income is tax-free.

One objection to fixed annuities is that once you start receiving income, you no longer have access to your investment, and there is no lump sum that could go to your heirs. Another objection is that, as life expectancies increase and people live longer, the income does not increase to offset the effects of inflation.

Lifetime payouts are determined by both life expectancy and current interest rates. For example, in mid-2009, MetLife was offering a fixed annuity that provided a lifetime income for husband and wife with a payout of about 6.4 percent. On $100,000, the payment was $6,413.95 a year, or $534.50 a month.

In mid-2012, with the drop in interest rates, the same fixed annuity payout is now $5,208.52, or $445.31 a month, a 19 percent decrease. Keep in mind that this payout includes both principal and interest. Thus, the nontaxable principal portion of the payout is $4,062.65, so the retiree would be paying taxes annually on only $1,145.87, a tax savings of more than $435 a year for someone in a 15 percent tax bracket.

Variable annuities, for their part, offer a guaranteed lifetime income, periodic payment increases, and death benefits. They are called variable because of the range of investment options available, chiefly in mutual funds. Thus the performance of a variable annuity will be tied to how well its investments perform during the ups and downs of the financial markets.

More than a decade ago, variable-annuity companies began adding new income-oriented features to make their offerings more attractive for retirement planning.

These features include a system of periodic increases in income, which can vary from one company to the next. First, most annuities will automatically "lock in" the highest anniversary value of the annuity. This means that the annual payment may start at $5,000 (5 percent of $100,000), but if the portfolio value were to increase to $110,000 the next year, the income would increase to $5,500 for life, even if the portfolio fell back to $100,000 the following year.

In addition to the lock-in, some annuities may provide that the value of a portfolio will be increased by the greater of a fixed percentage, such as 5 percent or 6 percent a year, or the value of the portfolio on its anniversary date. Once this number is determined, the next year's value is increased by either a higher portfolio value or the fixed percentage on top of the previous high—for example, on top of the $110,000. At the death of the first spouse, the remaining investment can be returned to the surviving spouse, or she can continue to draw regular payments at the same rate.

There are extra charges for these additional features.

There are a number of these newer-type variable annuities available today. Prudential, Lincoln, and Jackson National all have programs available, and all offer the features just discussed, although in slightly different fashions. Some variable annuities even have features that can help provide up to double the income in the event of a nursing-care need. However, they all offer income guarantees for life. An investor should be aware of the cost of these optional features, which could add 1 to 2 percent to the underlying cost of the annuity.

Anyone who is considering investing in an annuity should always review the fees and other charges involved, along with the many advantages associated with annuities.

A MANAGED DIVERSIFIED PORTFOLIO STRATEGY

The last decade has been a volatile one, with unusually low net returns in the stock market—near zero percent. However, this did not necessarily mean that a diversified portfolio would have had the same results. Indeed, several asset classes performed well over the past decade. While some would say that the stock market looks like a good value after a "lost decade," adding other asset classes to the portfolio could improve it by either lowering volatility or possibly increasing returns. Bonds, in particular Treasury bonds, are probably at or near the end of a 30-year bull market, which started with yields of roughly 15 percent. The 10-year bond yield has since dropped to less than 1.75 percent.

In any diversified portfolio, you want investments that do not all move in the same direction—that is, that do not either all go up or all go down depending on the economy. As a result, constructing this portfolio might start with a combination of the multisector bond portfolio and the high-quality dividend-paying stock portfolio described earlier.

In order to further diversify this portfolio, the retiree should consider adding other investments, such as international developed-country and emerging-market dividend-paying stocks and real estate investment trusts. International funds might include large, well-known companies such as GlaxoSmithKline (one of the largest prescription drug companies in the world), Siemens AG (a global electrical and engineering company), or Unilever (maker of Hellman's Mayonnaise and TRESemmé hair products). Currently, international stocks on average appear to have higher dividend rates than domestic stocks. However, an additional risk in investing internationally is the fluctuation of another country's currency in relation to our dollar. An investment that aims at the highest yields available in the world at a moderate risk level might also be considered. There are fewer choices that do all these things in just one investment. Mutual fund groups to check include J.P. Morgan, Oppenheimer & Co., and Thornburg Investment Management.

Typically, a fund with a diversified portfolio might have the following asset allocation: 25 percent global equity, 6.0 percent global REITs, 5.2 percent convertible bonds, 10.1 percent nonagency mortgages, 42.1 percent high-yield debt, 8.8 percent emerging-market debt, and 2.8 percent cash.

A MANAGED PORTFOLIO OF EXCHANGE-TRADED FUNDS

In the world of investing, one of the most significant innovations in recent years has been the creation of ETFs. ETFs have many features that appeal to investors. They can be bought and sold during the day like a stock and have a low average management fee, generally around 0.25 percent. Since most ETFs are based on stock, bond, commodity, real estate, and other popular indexes, ETFs offer an infinite variety of investment opportunities.

As with stocks and bonds, investors have a choice. They can invest in individual ETFs on their own, through their brokers, or they can turn their portfolios over to an ETF fund manager. A growing number of companies now manage money for clients by using ETFs as their investments. "The trend," Jack May said, "supports the idea that the asset allocation of a portfolio may be more important than specific stocks and bonds."

ETFs give a fund manager the flexibility to underweight or overweight different market sectors and to do so quickly by buying or selling broad index ETFs on the market at any time during the day. In addition, ETF managers are able to take advantage of market trends by using ETFs to invest in real estate investment trusts (REITs), commodities, or currencies. Finally, many are called tactical managers, which means that they actively invest their funds where they see the best values based on their research. Some ETF managers manage a suite of portfolios based on risk tolerance. For example, they may include portfolios ranging from all stocks to all bonds, with various combinations in between. These are typically well diversified, using a variety of asset classes to meet their objective. For example, one such manager runs a moderate portfolio that aims to be invested in roughly half stocks and half bonds and cash. In the second quarter of 2012, it was invested in 12 different ETFs, including 6 different bond ETFs, a commodity ETF, an international ETF, and domestic stock ETFs. This variety within a particular company makes it easier to invest according to your objective, as your investments can be moved between portfolios. Generally, these portfolios have higher minimum investments than mutual funds, with many starting at $25,000 or more.

Summing Up

These, then, are some of the choices available to investors for drawing income from their savings. If the choices appear weighted toward the conservative side, that seems appropriate during a time when the nation is struggling economically and the financial markets continue to be volatile.

The price for being too conservative is a much lower yield, as one can see from the near zero percent yields on bank accounts, Treasury bills, and money market accounts. This pushes retirees into the tough position of having to choose between increasing risk to achieve an income they can live on in retirement and accepting lower returns and thus lower incomes.

As we have seen over the past decade, investments that have worked in the past will not necessarily work in the future. Given the volatility and uncertainty in today's markets, you should carefully consider the alternatives for achieving your retirement income goals. Retirees should also consider their own willingness to take on risk as they weigh the advantages and disadvantages of the many investment alternatives available. Both your retirement income and your peace of mind may depend on it.

For More Information

BOOKS

Carlson, Robert C. *The New Rules of Retirement: Strategies for a Secure Future.* New York: Wiley, 2004.

Griffith, Bill, Jr. *Securing a Retirement Income for Life: Strategies for Managing, Protecting and Preserving Your Wealth,* 2nd ed. Washington, PA: W.E. Griffith Publications, 2009.

Hebeler, Henry K. *Getting Started in a Financially Secure Retirement.* Hoboken, NJ: Wiley, 2007.

FINANCIAL PLANNERS

You can get a list of Certified Financial Planners in your community from the Financial Planning Association. Go to its website—www.fpanet.org—and enter the name of your hometown, and the FPA web pages will give you the names and phone numbers of financial planners in your area. The FPA's phone number is 1-800-322-4237, and it is answered Monday through Friday from 9 a.m. to 6:30 p.m. EST.

Fee-only planners are represented by the National Association of Personal Financial Advisors. To obtain a list of fee-only planners in your home area, go to the organization's website, www.napfa.org, and provide the name and location of your home city. The web pages will give you a list of fee-only planners in nearby communities. NAPFA's phone number is 1-847-483-5400.

WEBSITES

Many of the nation's mutual funds operate websites that offer advice on investing and retirement. Some sites also have retirement "calculators" that will help you figure out how much you need to save for retirement or how long your money will last in retirement.

Some of the major mutual fund websites are found at these addresses:

American Century Investments: www.americancentury.com
Fidelity Investments: www.fidelity.com
MFS Investment Management: www.mfs.com
Oppenheimer Funds: www.oppenheimerfunds.com/investors
Putnam Investment Management: www.putnamfunds.com
T. Rowe Price Associates: www.troweprice.com
The Vanguard Group: www.vanguard.com

What Should I Do About Health Insurance?

As my wife, Sara, and I journey through our retirement years, few things are more important to us than our health insurance. As we have aged, we have become increasingly vulnerable to medical problems and the huge expenses that come with them. And we have both learned what it's like to need costly medical attention.

Shortly before we retired, I had a quadruple heart bypass operation, and Sara had surgery for breast cancer. Fortunately, our company health-insurance policies paid for most of our hospital and doctors' bills. It was a good thing they did. My medical costs totaled about $45,000, and Sara's were more than $20,000. Without our insurance, we'd have been in debt for years.

Then, when Sara developed Alzheimer's disease, the emotional and financial challenges were enormous. Fortunately, as I will explain in Decision 9, we had a long-term-care policy, which helped cover some of our expenses.

Going back a few years, when Sara and I first retired, we lost the health coverage we had had at our companies. So we migrated to Medicare, the federal insurance program that pays the hospital and doctors' bills of more than 47 million elderly and disabled Americans. At the same time, we signed up for a secondary insurance policy that was offered by GE, Sara's former employer, as a retirement benefit. This policy, which covers both of us, pays for some of the medical charges that are not covered by Medicare. If the GE policy had not been available, we would have bought a "Medigap" policy.

Why? Basically, because Medicare pays for most, but not all, of our hospital and doctors' bills. There is literally a gap between what hospitals and doctors charge us as patients and what Medicare will pay those providers for their services. Hence, the name Medigap for insurance policies that help close this gap by paying a portion of the bills that Medicare doesn't pay. If we didn't have this type of coverage, we would have to pay those costs ourselves, and that could add up to a lot of money over time.

Here's an example of how the Medicare system works when it comes to doctors' bills. Let's say I go to my doctor, and she charges me $100 for the visit. The doctor sends the bill to Medicare, which decides that the visit was worth only $80. Thus, $80 becomes what Medicare calls the *approved charge* for that visit. Under federal rules, Medicare requires that I pay a Part B deductible of $147 in 2013. This means that if I have not yet met this deductible during this calendar year, I will pay the entire cost of my visit to the doctor. But under Medicare rules, I will pay only the approved charge, or $80, for that visit. Once I have met the annual deductible, Medicare pays only 80 percent of an approved charge, which means that Medicare will pay the doctor 80 percent of $80, or $64. If you have a Medigap policy, it will pay the other 20 percent of the $80, or $16. If you don't have a Medigap policy, you will have to pay the $16 yourself.

That is the way Medicare deals with doctors' bills. But there are many other aspects of Medicare that current and future retirees need to know about. The bottom line is that Medicare is a giant government program that can be complicated and even frustrating at times. I will say that Sara and I have been generally satisfied with the way Medicare has handled *our* medical and hospital bills. However, if you are a retiree, you can depend on one thing: Medicare will play a major role in the quality and cost of your healthcare. In order to make the most of Medicare's benefits, you have to understand how the system works.

What Is Medicare?

Medicare, run by the Centers for Medicare and Medicaid Services (CMS), is a federal health-insurance program for people who are age 65 and older. It also covers people who are under 65 with certain disabilities and people who suffer from what is called end-stage renal disease. The Medicare definition of the latter is "permanent kidney failure treated with dialysis or a transplant."

There are four major parts to the Medicare program.

MEDICARE PART A

This is the part of Medicare that pays for hospital stays, medical services, home healthcare, hospice care, and limited care in skilled nursing facilities. People do not pay for Part A if they or a spouse have had 40 quarters—equal to 10 years—of Social Security earnings throughout their lifetime. People with less than 40 quarters may still qualify for Part A, but they will have to pay a monthly premium. In 2013, people who have 30 to 39 quarters pay $243 a month. For those with fewer than 30 quarters, the cost is $441 a month.

In 2013, hospital patients pay a $1,184 deductible for each hospital stay of 1 to 60 days. For days 61–90, they pay $296 a day. For days 91–150, they pay $592 a day. Those last 60 days are considered "lifetime" reserve days and can be used only once. Beyond 150 days, the patient pays all costs during a benefit period. A benefit period begins on the day your inpatient stay begins and ends 60 days after your discharge from the hospital or skilled nursing facility.

MEDICARE PART B

Medicare Part B pays for doctors' bills, medical tests, and medical equipment. For most people, Part B monthly premiums are deducted from their Social Security benefits. In 2013, the Medicare Part B premium is $104.90. High-income enrollees will pay more. In 2013, the premium is $146.90 for individuals with incomes above $85,000 and couples with incomes above $170,000. There are also three higher premium levels (see Table 8.1). The 2013 annual Medicare deductible is $147.

While Medicare pays for many hospital and medical services, there are a number of important items that it does not pay for. When my wife and I joined Medicare, we were surprised to discover that it does not pay for dental care, vision exams, eyeglasses (except one pair of glasses or contacts after cataract surgery), and hearing aids.

I wish I had known about the limitations of Medicare before I retired. When Sara and I were working, our company insurance plans covered dental care, routine physicals, and prescription drugs. Once we lost that coverage, we had to pick up those expenses ourselves—and items like gold crowns and hearing aids can be quite costly. As a result, our retirement budget should have

TABLE 8.1 2013 Monthly Premiums for Medicare Part B (Medical Insurance)

IF YOUR YEARLY INCOME IS		
FILE INDIVIDUAL TAX RETURN	FILE JOINT TAX RETURN	YOU PAY
$85,000 or below	$170,000 or below	$104.90*
$85,001-$107,000	$170,001-$214,000	$146.90*
$107,001-$160,000	$214,001-$320,000	$209.80*
$160,001-$214,000	$320,001-$428,000	$272.70*
Above $214,000	Above $428,000	$335.70*

* If you pay a late enrollment fee, this amount is higher.

Source: "Medicare and You," CMS Publication 10050, 2013.

included a couple of thousand dollars a year for medical, dental, and prescription drug expenses. Keep that in mind when you are drawing up your retirement budget.

Over the last several years, Medicare Part B has increasingly paid for preventive benefits such as mammograms, Pap smears, bone density tests, prostate tests, depression screening, HIV screening, obesity screening, and diabetes screening. Medicare has also introduced a "Welcome to Medicare" physical and annual wellness visits. The Affordable Care Act of 2010 eliminated cost sharing for many of these benefits to encourage more Medicare beneficiaries to take advantage of them.

One question I'm asked a lot is what changes are happening to Medicare because of the Affordable Care Act of 2010. Throughout this chapter, I highlight improvements in Medicare because of the new law—like reduced cost sharing for preventive benefits and reducing or eliminating the "doughnut hole" in Part D. However, the law also encourages changes in the delivery of medical care to beneficiaries. For example, Medicare has new initiatives to improve posthospital care at home to treat chronic medical conditions more effectively and prevent hospital readmission. Medicare is also working to develop "accountable care organizations" to provide incentives for doctors and hospitals to work together to improve care and lower the cost of medical care for older Americans.

Finally, and perhaps most important, the law makes health insurance available to individuals with medical conditions who are not yet eligible for Medicare based on their age and who cannot get health insurance through their employer. Beginning in 2014, the "exchanges" that are currently being set up in many states will provide health-insurance plans to these individuals that will, hopefully, be more affordable. The law provides subsidies for employers that continue to pay for health insurance or that subsidize the purchase of health insurance on the exchanges. Since many Americans without health insurance forgo medical care until they become Medicare-eligible, this change may encourage people to buy health insurance and enable them to obtain medical care earlier, before their condition becomes more serious—and more expensive for Medicare to cover when they do become eligible. I'm hopeful that some of the changes prompted by the Affordable Care Act will help limit the increasing cost of medical care while improving access to services for retirees and older Americans.

MEDICARE PART C

This is the part of Medicare that allows and even encourages Medicare recipients to get their care from private health plans. For more than a decade, the federal government has supported the creation of Medicare health maintenance organizations (HMOs), Medicare cost plans, demonstration/pilot programs, and the Program of All-Inclusive Care for the Elderly, known as the PACE program. The goal of these plans is to improve the quality of care and save money for the Medicare program and its beneficiaries. Not all Medicare options are available to beneficiaries in all parts of the country. To find out which plans might be available to you, you should consult the Medicare website at www.medicare.gov/find-a-plan/questions/home.aspx.

In 2003, when Congress passed the Medicare Prescription Drug, Improvement, and Modernization Act (MMA), it changed the name of the Medicare + Choice program to Medicare Advantage. As of 2011, approximately 25 percent of Medicare beneficiaries were enrolled in a Medicare Advantage plan. These plans have engendered some controversy because Medicare pays these plans more for each enrolled Medicare beneficiary than it would spend on average for that beneficiary if he were enrolled in traditional Medicare. As a result, the plans are able to provide additional benefits such as vision, hearing, or dental care that are not paid for by traditional Medicare. Although Congress reduced the disparity in the money paid to Medicare Advantage plans beginning in 2012, plans are able to continue to receive these higher payments by meeting quality improvement standards.

For some Medicare beneficiaries, Medicare Advantage plans save them money by lowering their out-of-pocket costs and offering additional benefits. These are generally younger, healthier beneficiaries who don't use much medical care. For other beneficiaries, joining a Medicare Advantage plan has cost them more money because the plan has higher deductibles or copayments than those charged by traditional Medicare. The Affordable Care Act of 2010 now prohibits Medicare Advantage plans from charging beneficiaries who need chemotherapy and dialysis more than the cost sharing under traditional Medicare.

In order to enroll in a Medicare Advantage plan, you must have Parts A and B of Medicare. You must continue to pay the Part B premium in addition to any premiums that the Medicare Advantage plan may charge. You must live in the plan's service area. Medicare Advantage plans (except Medicare special needs plans) can turn you down if you have end-stage renal disease

(ESRD)—that is, if you need kidney dialysis or have had a kidney transplant. However, if you join a Medicare Advantage plan and later develop ESRD, you can continue to be enrolled in that Medicare Advantage plan.

These are the main choices available under the Medicare Advantage program.

Medicare Health Maintenance Organizations (HMOs)

If you join an HMO, you will continue to pay Medicare your regular monthly premium. Medicare, in turn, will pay your HMO a specific sum for your healthcare, based on geographic and medical considerations. HMOs require their members to use doctors and hospitals in the HMO's network. In many HMOs, your primary-care physician serves as the person who refers you to specialists, and you generally can't see a specialist without a referral. So before you join a Medicare HMO, ask about the HMO's policies regarding referrals and whether the HMO has been sued for refusing to grant referrals. As noted, many HMOs offer hearing, vision, dental, and other benefits that are not covered by traditional Medicare. Typically, HMOs charge a monthly premium. Charges for office visits and other fees tend to be low, but if you go outside the network, you probably will have to pay the bill yourself. If your HMO has a "point-of-service" option, it may cover part of out-of-network costs.

Preferred-Provider Organizations (PPOs)

A Medicare PPO may have a broader network of doctors and hospitals than an HMO. As in an HMO, you pay your Part B premium to Medicare, which then pays the PPO for your care. Unlike HMOs, however, PPOs do not require their members to use the network's providers or to see a primary-care physician before going to a specialist. If your medical provider is part of the PPO network, the PPO pays a much larger portion of the bill; if your provider is not part of the network, the PPO pays much less.

Special Needs Plans (SNPs)

SNPs serve people who live in nursing homes or similar institutions or who require nursing care at home. They also serve people who are eligible for both Medicare and Medicaid or who have specific disabling conditions like diabetes, congestive heart failure, mental health conditions, or HIV/AIDS. An SNP provides case managers to develop a plan of care and to coordinate care for patients. Patients generally have to get their care from doctors and hospitals in the plan's network. SNPs must provide Part D Medicare prescription drug coverage.

These plans are intended to improve care for Medicare and Medicaid beneficiaries with special needs, primarily through improved coordination and continuity of care.

Medical Savings Account Plans (MSAs)

Medicare MSA plans have two parts. One is a health plan with a high deductible, which may be as much as $6,000 a year. The second is a bank account. Medicare gives your health plan a sum of money each year for your healthcare. The plan then deposits a portion of this money into your bank account. You may use this money to pay your medical bills during the year. Medicare rules limit the amount that doctors and other providers can charge you to the Medicare-approved amount. (See the discussion about the Medicare-approved amount earlier in the chapter.) For example, let's say I have an MSA with a high-deductible plan in which the annual deductible is $1,500. If I use a physician in the PPO network and the Medicare-approved amount is $80 instead of the physician's full charge of $100, I will pay only $80 for the doctor's visit out of my health savings account. (Remember, because this is a high-deductible plan, I will have to pay the full charge for my medical care until I reach $1,500 for the year.)

The amount your health plan puts into your bank account is likely to be less than your deductible. This means that if you use up the funds in your bank account, you will have to pay out of pocket before your insurance coverage begins. But if you are healthy and you don't need much medical care during the year, the plan payments into your account will add up, and you may find that you eventually have enough to pay this high deductible.

You may not contribute personally to your savings account, and you must use the money in the account only for medical care. (If you use the money for something other than medical care, you will have to pay taxes on the amount you spent.) MSA health plans may provide a network of physicians, but enrollees are not required to use network providers. MSA plans do not provide prescription drugs or a Part D prescription drug benefit.

The money you spend for Part A and Part B services will count toward your deductible. Once you have met your plan deductible for the year, your health plan pays 100 percent of your medical expenses. If you have money left in your account at the end of the year, it can remain there and grow tax-free.

Enrolling in, Leaving, and Changing Medicare Plans

People who join a Medicare Advantage plan generally are allowed to change plans or go back to traditional Medicare during the open enrollment period each year, which runs from October 15 to December 7. One change may be made between January 1 and February 14 each year. Special enrollment periods are provided if the plan discontinues serving your geographic area, if you move out of the plan's service area, or if your other health insurance ends.

MEDICARE PART D

In 2006, millions of beneficiaries were able to get federal financial help for the cost of their prescription drugs. In crafting the new Part D prescription drug law, Congress made fundamental changes in the Medicare program. Instead of letting the Medicare agency run the drug benefit the way it runs the hospital and medical portions of Medicare, Congress put the new drug benefit in the hands of private healthcare companies. The companies have considerable flexibility in designing their plans, but they must adhere to Medicare rules.

For most Medicare beneficiaries, enrollment in Part D, the prescription drug program, is voluntary—only individuals with both Medicare and Medicaid are required to sign up. Despite widespread concern about the cost of this new program, the program actually costs 30 percent less than anticipated. This is due to lower-than-expected enrollment (about 70 percent of Medicare beneficiaries were enrolled in the program in 2012), greater use of generic medications, and fewer new, more expensive drugs coming onto the market.[1] Generally, there are two ways for Medicare-eligible individuals to enroll a Part D plan—you can enroll in a "stand-alone" prescription drug plan (PDP) and get all your other medical benefits from original Medicare, or you can enroll in a Medicare Advantage plan, such as an HMO or PPO, where you will get prescription drug coverage and your regular Medicare benefits.

The Kaiser Family Foundation reported that there are more than 32 million Medicare beneficiaries enrolled in Part D in 2012, with about 20 million getting their prescriptions from stand-alone drug plans (PDPs) and almost 12 million from Medicare Advantage drug plans. The average monthly PDP premium is $30 in 2013.

Many retirees continue to get their drug coverage through their former employers and do not need to enroll in a Part D plan. Employers are free to purchase any health insurance, including prescription drug benefits, for their employees and retirees and

---

[1] Jack Hoadley, "Medicare Part D Spending Trends: Understanding Key Drivers and the Role of Competition," Kaiser Family Foundation Issue Brief, May 2012.

may reduce or discontinue these benefits at any time. To encourage employers to continue their retiree health plans, an employer may receive a federal subsidy to help cover retiree drug costs from $310 to $6,300 per year.

In order to receive this subsidy, employers must provide a prescription drug benefit that is "at least as good as" the Part D benefit and must notify their retirees by letter whether their plans are considered, in an actuarial sense, to be at least as good as the basic Medicare drug plan. Retirees should save that letter or document. It will help them prove that they did have equal coverage—or what Medicare calls *credible coverage*—in the event that the retiree leaves the drug plan or the employer discontinues the coverage and the retiree needs to purchase a Part D plan.

That's important because if the retiree then applies for drug coverage under a Part D plan, being able to show proof of previous credible coverage will help the retiree avoid a late-enrollment penalty.

If a retiree with employer-provided drug coverage does not receive such a letter or document, the retiree should check with the employer's human resources department. Not all drug plans provided by employers will meet the credible coverage test.

The healthcare reform law, known as the Affordable Care Act, that became law in 2010 made two important changes in Part D. First, the law gradually eliminates the "doughnut hole" or coverage gap (discussed later in this chapter) beginning in 2011 and concluding in 2020, providing greater coverage for drugs and limiting the copayments to 25 percent of the cost of the drug. Second, the law requires high-income Medicare beneficiaries to pay higher Part D premiums, as they now do for Part B. This change will increase Part D premiums for approximately 1.2 million Medicare beneficiaries in 2013. The premiums for Part D for people with different incomes are given in Table 8.2.

TABLE 8.2 2012 Monthly Premiums for Medicare Part D (Medical Insurance)

| IF YOUR YEARLY INCOME IN 2010 WAS | | |
FILE INDIVIDUAL TAX RETURN	FILE JOINT TAX RETURN	YOU PAY
$85,000 or below	$170,000 or below	Your plan premium
$85,001–$107,000	$170,001–$214,000	$11.60 + your plan preimium
$107,001–$160,000	$214,001–$320,000	$29.90 + your plan preimium
$160,001–$214,000	$320,001–$428,000	$48.10 + your plan preimium
Above $214,000	Above $428,000	$66.40 + your plan preimium

Source: "Medicare and You," CMS Publication 10050, 2012.

Choosing a Plan

For the majority of people enrolling in Medicare, finding the right prescription drug plan is something of a challenge. It can be a confusing process because in most states across the country, individuals can choose from more than 37 plans with different premiums, different deductibles, and different drug coverage. It is very difficult to determine which plan best fits your needs.

Fortunately, help is available at www.medicare.gov. Click on "Compare Drug and Health Plans." You will have two options: a general search by zip code or a personalized search where you enter specific information on the secure website for more accurate price information. With either search, it is helpful to have a list of the specific prescriptions that you take. Entering your prescriptions will give you more precise information regarding the costs of the plans that are available to you. You can save even more money if you are willing to switch to a generic drug if one is available instead of a brand-name drug.

You will find that premiums will vary depending on your zip code and the details of a specific plan, including the amount of the deductible, which could not exceed $320 in 2013.

In any given plan, the cost of individual drugs will depend on what drugs are available, how they are priced, and the plan's rules concerning the use of generics versus brand-name drugs. You will find that some plans have a higher deductible and charge a lower monthly premium, while others charge a higher premium but have little or no deductible.

Part D enrollees must also consider whether to purchase a stand-alone prescription drug plan (PDP) or enroll in a Medicare Advantage plan that offers the specific drugs they need and includes their physician in the plan network. All plans must cover at least two drugs in each therapeutic category of covered Part D drugs, but persons enrolling in drug plans are advised to find out if the particular drugs they need will be available to them.

Health insurance expert L. Sue Andersen of Silver Spring, Maryland, offers this advice:

The bottom line is, if you do not have a prescription drug plan through a current employment health plan or a retirement health plan, you should probably sign up for a Part D plan. Obviously, if you choose a Medicare Advantage plan, check to be sure they cover the drugs you need. And, if you don't enroll in a Medicare Advantage plan, you still should enroll in a stand-alone PDP plan because sooner or later you will have high prescription drug costs, and you may have to pay a penalty to enroll later. If you don't take many prescription drugs when you first sign up, at least enroll in a plan with a low or zero deductible so you can take full advantage of the $2,600 subsidy provided by Medicare in 2011 for any drugs you do take. And if you have high prescription drug costs that exceed the annual limit for your out-of-pocket costs (approximately $4,700 in 2012), you will qualify for catastrophic coverage, which *pays most of your drug costs until the end of each year. As mentioned, individuals who are enrolled in Part D in 2013 pay an estimated average monthly premium of $30. Generally speaking, enrollees also pay a $320 deductible in 2012. Enrollment in Part D is voluntary. However, persons who delay enrollment will pay a 1 percent lifetime premium penalty for each month—or about 37 cents in 2012 if they delay after their enrollment deadline.*

Part D enrollees are allowed to change their drug plans each year from October 15 to December 7, to be effective January 1. You should consider reevaluating your drug plan each year—the benefits and costs of each plan change from year to year, so the plan you choose this year may not be the one that fits your needs next year. Finally, low-income beneficiaries can get "extra help" in paying premiums and deductibles. According to CMS, 8.2 million people were eligible for financial help with Part D expenses if their annual incomes in 2011 were below $16,245 for a single person or $21,855 for a married couple. Slightly higher income levels may apply if you help support relatives who live with you or if you live in Alaska or Hawaii. The limit on financial resources was $12,640 for an individual and $25,260 for a married couple. Resources include savings, stocks and bonds, and real estate other than the value of a person's home. All of these figures may change from year to year.

The Mary Jones Story

Let's consider how Part D would work for Mary Jones, who signs up for a stand-alone PDP in 2012. Mary pays an estimated $39.40 monthly premium, or $472.80 a year. When Mary begins to order drugs under the Part D plan, she pays for the first $320 worth of prescriptions herself; that is her deductible.

After meeting her $320 deductible, Mary begins to get help with her drug expenses. On the next $2,930 worth of drugs, Mary pays 25 percent of the cost, or $726.50. The government, through her plan, pays the other 75 percent, or $2,203.50. After that, Mary hits the controversial gap in coverage that is often referred to as the "doughnut hole." The gap means that Mary must pay the next $3,728 in drug expenses herself. At that point, Mary has paid a $320 deductible, $727 in co-pays, and $3,653 out of pocket, for a total of $4,700. If you add the $2,203.50 that Medicare paid initially, this means that Mary's drug spending totaled $6,903. Once Mary spends that amount for her prescriptions, she will have reached the "catastrophic" level, after which Medicare and her plan will pay 95 percent of any additional drug expenses, while she will pay only 5 percent.

Thus there are two ways of looking at Part D and how helpful it is to Medicare recipients. Before Mary reached the $6,658, or catastrophic, spending level, she spent $4,700, or 70.6 percent of the cost of her prescriptions. If you add the $473 yearly cost for her monthly premiums, her total outlay was $5,173, or 77 percent of her drug costs. Thus, Part D paid only about 23 percent of her drug costs. On the other hand, if Mary had had no other prescription coverage, she would have had to pay 100 percent of the cost herself.

Applying for Medicare

Although I didn't retire and go on Medicare Part B until I was 69, I signed up for Medicare Part A when I turned 65. If you continue to work after you reach 65 and continue to have company health insurance, as I did, you should take Part A at 65 and wait until you retire to sign up for Part B. Part A is free for most people, so it won't cost you anything if you do sign up while you are still enrolled in your employment health plan. That's fine with the folks at SSA and Medicare, who want people to sign up when they first become eligible. However, as noted, they make exceptions for people who continue to work after they are 65 or their full retirement age, which is slowly moving up to 67.

If you do enroll in Part A while you continue to work and have your employment health insurance, you may have some difficulty figuring out which insurance pays your medical bills—Medicare or your employment plan. For most people who work past 65, your employment health insurance pays first if your employer has 20 or more full-time employees. Medicare will pay *after* your employment health insurance. If your employer has fewer than 20 employees, Medicare pays first.

If, like many people, you decide to retire when you reach your full retirement age and begin drawing your Social Security benefits, you must enroll in Part A at that time. You should also sign up for Part B and Part D at that time. You can notify the SSA anytime before you stop working or within eight months after you stop working that you want Medicare, and your Medicare benefits will begin almost immediately.

Don't delay. Delay could cost you money. If you wait 12 months or more to sign up for Medicare, your monthly premiums will go up. Part B premiums will rise 10 percent for each 12 months in which you could have enrolled but didn't. The increase in the Part A premium, if you have to pay a premium, will be 10 percent no matter how late you are. To enroll in Medicare, call the SSA number: 1-800-772-1213.

Choosing a Medigap Policy

We come now to the ins and outs of choosing a Medigap policy, which, as I've mentioned, is intended to fill the gap between your medical expenses and what Medicare pays. At this point, it won't surprise you to learn that choosing a Medigap policy is a decision that can be rather complicated and requires a careful study of the 11 standard policies that insurers are permitted to sell to consumers after June 1, 2010. More than 1,300 health insurers offer Medigap policies, but they do not all sell policies in all states.

Almost 30 percent of Medicare beneficiaries have retirement health insurance through their former employers and do not need a Medigap policy because the retirement plan picks up the gaps in Medicare coverage.

In 2010, Congress made some significant changes in current and future Medigap policies. Two distinct trends in the Medigap insurance market are reflected in the 2010 offerings. First, there is a greater emphasis on policies that have higher cost-sharing features but have lower premiums. Second, with the advent of the Medicare Part D prescription drug plan, Medigap plans no longer provide drug coverage.

In 1990, Congress standardized the various types of Medigap policies to address widespread confusion among Medicare beneficiaries regarding which policies they needed and widespread abuse by many insurance agents who sought to sell more policies. Insurance companies were allowed to sell only 10 standard policies, some of which provided coverage for prescription drugs. In the 2010 redesign, after additions and subtractions, there are 11 benefit packages that insurance companies can offer to consumers (see Table 8.3). Each of the standardized plans has a letter name—Plan A, C, or F, for example—which, of course, makes it even more difficult to distinguish a Medigap plan from the parts of Medicare that we just discussed. Plans C and F were the most popular Medigap plan choices for most Medicare beneficiaries; however, by 2015, the Affordable Care Act requires that individuals pay some cost sharing out of pocket that they now do not do.

Individuals who hold older policies will be allowed to keep those policies. Those policies that included prescription drug benefits were required to strip out these benefits. If a current

TABLE 8.3 Benefits of Medicare Supplement Plans

MEDICARE SUPPLEMENT INSURANCE PLANS (MEDIGAP)

BENEFITS	A	B	C	D	F*	G	K	L	M	N
Medicare Part A coinsurance and hospital costs (up to an additional 365 days after Medicare benfits are used)	✓	✓	✓	✓	✓	✓	✓	✓	✓	✓
Medicare part B coinsurance or copayment	✓	✓	✓	✓	✓	✓	50%	75%	✓	✓**
Blood (first 3 pints)	✓	✓	✓	✓	✓	✓	50%	75%	✓	✓
Part A hospice care coinsurance or copayment	✓	✓	✓	✓	✓	✓	50%	75%	✓	✓
Skilled nursing facility care coinsurance			✓	✓	✓	✓	50%	75%	✓	✓
Medicare Part A deductible		✓	✓	✓	✓	✓	50%	75%	50%	✓
Medicare Part B deductible			✓		✓					
Medicare Part B excess charges					✓	✓				
Foreign travel emergency (up to plan limits)			✓	✓	✓	✓			✓	✓
							Out-of-pocket limit			
							$4,540	$2,320		

*For effective dates on or after June 1, 2010.

Plan F also offers a high-deductible plan. If you choose this option, this means that you must pay for Medicare-covered costs (coinsurance, copayments, and deductibles) up to the deductible amount of $2,000 in 2011 before your policy pays anything.

**Plan N pays 100 percent of the Part B coinsurance, except for a copayment of up to $20 for some office visits and up to a $50 copayment for emergency room visits that don't result in an inpatient admission.

Source: "Medicare and You," Publication 10050 2012 CMS.

policyholder wants to move to one of the newer policies, she will be allowed to do so. It will be up to each insurance company to decide whether it wants to require a physical examination. That exam could result in the denial of the application or limits being placed on the coverage of the new policy.

The current Medigap lineup eliminates the old Plans E, H, I, and J. Two new plans, M and N, were added for 2010. Plan M provides 50 percent coverage of the Medicare Part A deductible but covers 100 percent of the Part B deductible. Plan N covers the Part A and Part B deductibles but adds a new copayment structure of $20 for each physician visit and up to $50 for each emergency room visit.

What is most important for consumers to understand is that policies in each letter group, Plan C, for example, must offer the same benefits, no matter which insurance company issues the policy. Remember, too, that Medigap policies will pay only for items that Medicare covers. If Medicare won't pay for a medical procedure, neither will a Medigap policy.

Also bear in mind that not all companies sell all 11 policies, and not all policies are sold in all 50 states. You can buy only a plan that has been approved by regulators in your state. And, by the way, it is illegal for an insurance company to sell a Medigap policy to a person who is on Medicaid or who already has a Medigap policy.

When you are shopping for Medigap insurance, it is important to compare premiums because there are great variations in the amounts that different companies charge *for the same coverage*. If you decide you want to buy a Plan C policy, you will get the same policy regardless of which company you buy it from—but you may pay more for it depending on the way the company prices the policy.

The key to price shopping is to understand that companies use three different methods to calculate annual premiums.

Companies may base their policy prices on "attained age," "issue age," or community rating.

ATTAINED AGE

With a policy based on attained age, the premium is based upon your current age and increases automatically as you grow older. Typically, these plans will appear to be less expensive when you are younger, but they may cost considerably more in later years. The vast majority of policies sold in this country are based on attained age.

COMMUNITY RATED

A few companies charge the same premium for all policyholders regardless of age. These policies, called community-rated, may be more expensive initially but less expensive in the long run. For people over age 75, a policy with no age rating may be less costly than one based on attained age. You should compare policies based on what they are likely to cost you over the next 5 or 10 years. Be alert for discounts that some policies make available to couples or nonsmokers.

ISSUE AGE

With policies of this type, the premium is set when you buy the policy. You continue to pay the premium required of a person of the same age you were when the policy was issued. For example, if you buy a policy at age 65, you will always pay the rate the company charges people who are 65, regardless of your advancing age. However, the rate for 65-year-olds could go up.

CAN YOUR MEDIGAP APPLICATION BE TURNED DOWN?

One of the most important things for future retirees to know is that there is a one-time open-enrollment period for buying

Medigap insurance. If you apply for a Medigap policy within six months of signing up for Part B, you cannot be turned down, according to health insurance expert L. Sue Andersen. However, after the six-month period, the company may ask you to fill out an application that asks questions about your health. This is called *medical underwriting.*

If you have a medical condition, said Andersen, the insurance company may deny your application or may accept your application but refuse to cover your "preexisting" medical condition for a period of up to six months. Under current law, Andersen noted, if an insurance company imposes such a waiting period, it must reduce the period by one month for each month you had coverage under another health-insurance policy before your application. This prior coverage is called *creditable coverage.* If you had more than six months of prior coverage, the Medigap health plan cannot refuse to cover your preexisting condition.

For people who work after age 65 and for younger people who receive Medicare, there are special open-enrollment rules.

WHAT DOES MEDIGAP COST?

Medigap policies are generally more expensive and offer less healthcare coverage than retirement health insurance that you may have available from your former employer. For this reason, if you have retirement health coverage, keep it and don't get a Medigap policy. If you don't have a retirement health benefit or if it ends, it pays to shop around for a Medigap policy. Prices vary widely for policies that provide the same coverage. So where can you get a list of insurance companies that sell Medigap policies and the prices of those policies?

A good place to start is with the state insurance department in the state where you live or by contacting the State Health

Insurance Assistance Program (SHIP) sponsored by the insurance or aging services office in your state. An insurance company cannot sell you a Medigap policy unless that policy has been approved for sale in your state. Thus, state insurance departments are likely to be able to provide you with information about companies that sell Medigap policies in your state and about the prices of those policies.

The Maryland Insurance Administration, for instance, has a list of companies that sell Medigap policies in the state and the prices they charge. The 2012 list shows that for 65-year-olds, Plan A policies sold for as little as $1,038 and as much as $2,580 a year. Plan F policies sold for as low as $1,768 and as high as $2,846 a year.

Nationally, prices vary from state to state, and, as mentioned, not all companies sell all policies in all states. A 2009 national survey by TheStreet.com Ratings, Inc., of Jupiter, Florida, showed that Plan A policies for a 70-year-old female sold for as little as $423 and as much as $5,909. For Plan F policies, the lowest price was $587, and the highest was $9,021. Given these wide variations in price, it is obviously important to shop around and carefully compare the cost of the Medigap policies that are available in your state.

RETURNING TO MEDIGAP

People who join Medicare HMOs and other Medicare Advantage plans do not need Medigap policies. But once you give up your policy, it may be difficult to get it back. Or, if you can get new Medigap coverage, it may not be the policy you want. However, Medicare points out that there are at least three limited situations in which people who have joined Medicare HMOs may be able to get new Medigap policies or retrieve the ones they had before they joined a managed-care plan:

- You can get your Medigap policy back if you lost your health coverage through no fault of your own, as when your HMO quit the business.

- You can get your policy back if you joined an HMO for the first time but decided to leave within a year.

- If you were new to Medicare when you joined an HMO and thus did not have a Medigap policy, you can probably get any policy you want if you decide to leave the HMO within a year.

- If you had a retirement health plan that ended, you may get a Medigap plan or join a Medicare Advantage plan.

To get those protections, you have to apply for a Medigap policy within 63 calendar days after your previous coverage ends. To see how the rules may apply to you, call 1-800-633-4227 and talk to a Medicare customer service representative.

For More Information

WEBSITES

The official Medicare website, www.medicare.gov, contains basic information about Medicare and its many features. It allows you to compare health insurance policies and nursing homes. You can also read, print, and order booklets published by the Centers for Medicare and Medicaid Services.

The Kaiser Family Foundation website, www.kff.org/, contains detailed information about Medicare. From the Home Page left side, click on the Medicare link in the Browse by Topic column. The Medicare section contains numerous publications about Medicare programs, including "Talking About Medicare: Your Guide to Understanding the Program: Welcome—April 2012."

TELEPHONE NUMBERS

Call 1-800-MEDICARE (1-800-633-4227) for information and publications. TTY users should call 1-877-486-2048.

PUBLICATIONS

Medicare publishes dozens of helpful booklets, including:

"Medicare & You" (CMS Pub. 10050)
"Choosing a Medigap Policy: A Guide to Health Insurance for People with Medicare" (CMS Pub. 02110)
"Publications for Your Medicare Beneficiaries" (CMS Pub. 11034)
"Your Guide to Medicare Prescription Drug Coverage" (CMS Pub. 11109)
"Your Guide to Choosing a Nursing Home" (CMS Pub. 02174)
"Medicare and Home Health Care" (CMS Pub. 10969)

For a comprehensive list of Medicare publications, go to the Medicare home page (http://www.medicare.gov/default.aspx). Click on Help & Resources for the drop-down menu. Select Publications. View All Publications lists all Medicare publications to date.

Consumer health information websites:

Medicare Rights Center: www.medicarerights.org
Kaiser Family Foundation: www.kff.org
National Council on Aging: www.ncoa.org

What Should I Do to Prepare for an Illness That Requires Long-Term Care?

In a previous edition of this book, I began this chapter with these sentences: "I don't know what scares you about growing older, but I can tell you what scares me. It's the idea that my health or the health of my wife, Sara, might deteriorate to the point where one of us would have to become a resident of a nursing home for an extended period of time." When I wrote that, little did I know that in 2007, Sara would be afflicted by Alzheimer's disease, a particularly cruel malady for which there is currently no cure. Over a period of several years, Sara's condition worsened, and when she was no longer able to attend to any of her personal needs, she was placed in a residential nursing facility where she could get full-time care. To watch this once-accomplished wife, mother, and business executive lose her cognitive abilities broke the collective hearts of her husband, children, and grandchildren.

As you know, *How to Retire Happy* is a book about how to prepare for retirement. My goal is to give you the information and tools you will need for a successful retirement. But as I think about what has happened to my wife, I ask myself: "What can I possibly do to help my readers prepare for a similar illness that may strike them or their families?"

I do not have an answer to that overwhelming question. But I hope it may help my readers if I describe the unexpected challenges that awaited me and that may await them.

The Alzheimer's story frequently begins with a diagnosis called *mild cognitive impairment* (MCI). Alzheimer's is a disease that afflicts 5.4 million adults in the United States, according to the Alzheimer's Association.

During the first few years of Sara's illness, we took her to a series of doctors and specialists, only to find that even the most knowledgeable doctors had no answers for us. Repeatedly, my children and I had our hopes for medical help shattered as the doctors merely shrugged their shoulders.

As Sara's need for hands-on care increased, we hired a home healthcare aide. Up to then, I had been Sara's only caregiver. When the aide arrived each morning, she helped bathe and dress Sara. Not used to a stranger's attention, Sara frequently fussed with the aide, making for an unpleasant situation. The aide, who was a Maryland Certified Nursing Assistant, worked for a licensed agency that charged us $21 an hour. Although we had a long-term-care policy through CNA Insurance, the policy paid only $55 a day for home care, but we were spending $168 a day for an eight-hour shift. Our bills quickly mounted up.

Several months later, when it was clear that Sara needed to be in a facility where she would get full-time care, I began to look around at what was available in suburban Maryland, where I live. I quickly began to feel terribly lost. I knew I had to make a decision. But how? There were dozens of nursing and assisted-living facilities in the area, ranging from showy, corporate-owned palaces with hundreds of patients to small side-of-the-road group homes with space for 15 people.

The prices ranged from $7,000 to $12,000 a month for the more luxurious places and $3,000 to $4,000 a month for the smaller, less elaborate facilities. The homes differed not only in size and in price, but also in whether they had doctors or nurses on duty and their ratio of staff to patients. How could I decide in a short time where Sara would get the best care? The experience was baffling and frightening.

Eventually, we met a care manager who was highly recommended and, after getting favorable reports from the relatives of her other patients, we placed Sara in the facility at a cost of $4,000 a month. We paid $8,000 out of pocket during the 60-day period while we waited for our long-term-care insurance policy to kick in. After that, CNA Insurance paid $130 a day, or about $3,900 a month. Still unsure of what I had done, I visited Sara almost every day so that I could make my own appraisal of her condition and the care that she was receiving.

It is sometimes said that the health of the caregiver may be more at risk than that of the Alzheimer's patient. From my experience, I can tell you that caregivers are subject to enormous levels of stress. However, if caregivers are wise, they will take steps to preserve their own mental and physical health. One way to do this, I find, is to devise a daily schedule that allows you to spend time with your loved one but also allows you to take part in social and community activities. Friends are especially important because they can help you maintain your emotional balance at a time when your life seems to be spinning out of control. Just remember, if you want to be around to help care for your loved one, you have to maintain your own health.

Our Long-Term-Care Policy

The one bright spot in Sara's illness was the fact that we had bought long-term-care insurance policies. This meant that, if we became ill, we would be partially protected from the devastating costs of nursing home care. Sara and I bought our policies when the *Washington Post* offered them to its employees some years ago. The group policy was issued by CNA Insurance. Originally, our policy paid $110 a day for nursing home care and $55 a day for home care, with a maximum total benefit of $220,000 each, which equates to 5.5 years in a nursing home. My policy, which I took out at the age of 64, costs $1,089.48 a year. Sara's policy, which she took out at the age of 62, originally cost $945.96 a year but was raised to $1,724.36 because her benefits were later upgraded to $130 a day for nursing home care and $65 a day for home care. Her maximum total benefit rose to $260,000—which also equates to 5.5 years. However, once Sara began to draw regular monthly benefit payments from CNA, she no longer had to pay premiums.

BENEFITS OF A LONG-TERM-CARE POLICY

Buying a long-term-care policy makes a lot of sense when you look at the expense of nursing home care.

Without a long-term-care policy, you face the very real threat that you could be wiped out financially by the cost of care.

The national average fee for a private room in a nursing home is $239 a day, or a whopping $87,235 a year, according to a 2011 survey by the MetLife Mature Market Institute. In the Washington, DC, area where I live, private rooms cost an average of $315 a day, or $114,975 a year, according to MetLife.

But what happens if you are so ill that you have to stay in a nursing home indefinitely? It's no secret. Inevitably, you'll eventually go on Medicaid, a medical program for the poor that allows you to remain in a nursing home without paying. But to become eligible for Medicaid, you have to pay the nursing home until you virtually run out of money. Becoming eligible for Medicaid to pay for long-term care is a tricky business—you would be well advised to consult a lawyer if you or a member of your family has assets and is likely to need nursing home care.

Additionally, many people who need enough help that they can no longer remain in their own home often do not actually need nursing home care—rather, they need assistance with meal preparation, some assistance with and reminders about taking medications, and, more generally, just someone to make sure of their safety on a daily basis. Most of these people need the level of care provided in an assisted-living facility. Neither Medicare nor Medicaid pays for the costs of an assisted-living facility. However, a long-term-care policy may help to pay for assisted-living care.

Buying a Long-Term-Care Policy

Buying a long-term-care policy is a lot like buying a car. The more bells and whistles you want, the more it costs. You can get a policy that pays $100, $150, or even $200 a day for nursing home care. As the benefits go up, so does the cost of the policy. However, consider how the policy is written. You need to understand how the policy will be administered, with an emphasis on the reputation of the underwriter.

If you're interested in long-term-care insurance, remember that the younger you are when you buy a policy, the less it will cost per year.

After I retired, I did some research on long-term-care policies. The more I looked at the provisions of my policy, the more things I wished I could change. For instance, we do not have

171

inflation protection. Without it, we will still be getting a daily benefit of $110 to $130 when nursing homes in the Washington area cost considerably more. There are other aspects of our policies that I also dislike, including the following.

THE WAITING PERIOD

The policy has a 60-day waiting period for nursing home benefits and a 15-day wait for home-care benefits. That means that if I had to go to a nursing home, I would have to pay for the first 60 days myself. In Sara's case, that cost was $8,000. LTC experts point out that all policies have some kind of waiting period. Without the waiting period, they say, the cost of the policy would be prohibitive.

WAIVING THE PREMIUM

The insurance company says that if I go to a nursing home, I can stop paying the premiums on my long-term-care policy. That sounds generous, but wait—that benefit also doesn't kick in until I've been in a nursing home for 60 days.

GETTING PAID

To collect under my policy, I would need to show that I have a "qualifying impairment," meaning that I am unable to perform by myself at least two of the so-called activities of daily living. These activities include eating, dressing, going to the toilet, bathing, moving from the bed to the chair, and managing medications.

Who decides whether I can or can't do these things? The insurance company, of course. The policy says that the company will consult with my doctors and caregivers, but it's free to have its own doctor examine me to see whether I have a qualifying impairment.

HIGHER RATES

The policy says that the company can't raise my individual premium, but it can raise the rate of everybody in my class—that is to say, everybody who is my age and who bought the same policy when I did years ago. Thus far, our rates have stayed about the same. But rates do go up from time to time at various companies.

One other thing that our policy lacks is any sort of "nonforfeiture" clause. The clause comes into effect if you stop paying your premiums after paying them for a specified number of years. It assures you that you will still receive a portion of your long-term-care benefits.

While my CNA policy has the aforementioned negatives, it also has some relatively attractive features, including the following.

HOME HEALTHCARE

The insurer will pay for home healthcare services from a variety of therapists, registered or licensed nurses, home healthcare aides, or medical social workers. Better yet, the insurer also will pay for "homemaker services, such as cooking, cleaning, laundering, organizing bills for payment, and running errands." There is, however, one small catch: the person that you hire to provide home healthcare services must be a registered or licensed nurse or an aide who works for an organization that is licensed, registered, or accredited by either the state or a professional organization. While in some respects this requirement is a good one—the agency provides some assurance that the person has appropriate training and experience—the cost to you is higher than it would be if you could hire someone who advertised in a local newspaper or was otherwise not affiliated with any agency.

ALTERNATIVE PLAN OF CARE

My policy provides that, if I need them, the company will pay for special treatments and devices if the doctors and the insurer agree that they would be medically beneficial. While Medicare pays for some medical equipment for your home, such as hospital beds, it does not pay for other equipment that may be paid for by the long-term-care insurance.

What Do Long-Term-Care Policies Cost?

The cost of a long-term-care policy depends on several factors: your age, your health, where you live, and the features included in the policy. But, in a larger sense, the price you pay also will reflect the high cost of long-term care in the United States.

According to a 2011 survey by the MetLife Mature Market Institute, the national average fee for a private room in a nursing home is $239 a day or $87,235 a year. This was a 4.4 percent increase over 2010. A semiprivate room in 2011 costs $214 a day, or $78,110 a year. This may not include additional expenses incurred by residents, such as managing medications.

Assisted-living facilities are also quite costly. In 2011, the national average monthly rate was $3,477, or $41,724 a year, according to MetLife. Again, this may not include additional expenses incurred by residents.

MetLife studies also found that, in 2011, it cost $21 an hour to hire home health aides provided by a home-care agency. An eight-hour shift thus would cost $168, or $1,176 for a seven-day week.

Interestingly, statistics show that only about 20 percent of people who need long-term care are residents of nursing homes. The other 80 percent live at home or in assisted-living facilities.

Given the cost of long-term care, it is no surprise that the prices of new long-term-care insurance policies have been on the rise. It is also no surprise that many individuals have bought insurance to protect their savings.

To get a realistic look at the costs of long-term-care policies, I talked with Arthur Stein, a Certified Financial Planner in Bethesda, Maryland. Stein has sold long-term-care insurance for 22 years.

Stein showed me the cost estimates and other details of policies issued by three insurance companies: Mutual of Omaha, MassMutual, and Genworth Financial (a spin-off from General Electric). These policies were for $200 a day maximum for nursing homes, assisted-living facilities, and home care for three years, or the equivalent of $219,000.

Stein and I looked at the prices for couples at two age levels: 62 years of age and 52 years of age.

The monthly premiums for Mr. and Mrs. Older Couple were Mutual of Omaha, $699; MassMutual, $756; and Genworth, $540.

The monthly premiums for Mr. and Mrs. Younger Couple were Mutual of Omaha, $591; MassMutual, $592; and Genworth, $349.

These policies include a 20 to 40 percent discount for couples compared to the rates for single individuals. They do not include preferred health discounts.

What would the couples get for their money if they were to buy these policies?

For each spouse, the policies would provide the following: $200 per day for care in nursing homes or assisted-living facilities and $200 a day for home care. The policies would pay for three years—the equivalent of $219,000—but would allow each spouse to share as needed from their pool of eight years of coverage.

The policies also would provide inflation protection at a rate of 5 percent compounded annually, meaning that the initial $200-a-day coverage would rise by 5 percent each year without any increase in premiums. Each policy includes a 90-day waiting period for benefits.

All three companies allow policyholders to stop paying their premiums when their waiting period ends and they begin receiving benefits.

In order to receive their daily benefit, policyholders would have to be unable to perform two out of six activities of daily living (ADLs) or suffer from cognitive impairment.

While physical exams generally are not required before someone is approved for a policy, Stein said, an insurance company would want to see the results of a physical before paying benefits.

All three policies also would provide home-care help from health aides and other caregivers.

Stein noted that before buying a policy, individuals should ask about a company's financial ratings from national rating agencies. A company's ability to pay claims—not only at the present time, but years into the future—is an important factor for consumers to consider when shopping for a policy.

The three policies that Stein discussed all include a "contingent nonforfeiture" feature. This means, Stein said, that if a company raises the cost of a policy and the policyholder is unable to pay the increase, the policyholder can reduce her benefit so that the savings approximately equal the amount of the cost increase.

This goes part of the way toward addressing what I see as one of the discouraging features of long-term-care insurance: that people can pay their premiums for many years, but if they stop paying because the company raises its rates, or for any other reason, their policy lapses and they lose everything that they have paid over the years.

It can be argued, of course, that long-term-care insurance is really no different from auto, fire, or disability insurance. When you stop paying on those policies, you also lose your coverage. But it seems to me that long-term-care insurance should be in a separate category, given the near certainty that an individual will need his benefits eventually.

In any event, many more individuals might be willing to buy long-term-care insurance if they could expect some return of their money when they can no longer afford the premiums.

I also believe that sales of long-term-care insurance in this country would be encouraged if insurance companies could find a way to turn these policies into savings vehicles—especially for those who pay for 25 or 30 years and never use the benefits.

The Federal Option

Many Americans may be eligible for another long-term-care insurance option: The Federal Long Term Care Insurance Program (FLTCIP). The program is open to federal and U.S. Postal Service employees, annuitants, and active and retired members of the uniformed services. Coverage is also currently available to their qualified relatives including spouses, parents (including in-laws and stepparents), adult children, and same-sex domestic partners, so long as underwriting standards are met. For more information on this program go to www.LTCfeds.com.

Who Needs Long-Term-Care Insurance?

That brings us to a basic question about long-term-care insurance: how do you decide whether to buy a policy? The answer, I find, depends on your financial and family situations.

Let's talk first about your family situation. If you become seriously ill and you have a spouse or a child who would be willing or able to be an active caregiver, you may have a good chance of remaining at home instead of going to a nursing home. Thus, you may not need nursing home benefits, although a policy providing home health benefits might be useful. However, there is no guarantee that your spouse or children, devoted as they might be, could care for you for very long. When people develop Alzheimer's disease or other serious medical problems, as I discovered, there may be no choice but to seek the 24-hour care that's available in a nursing home.

What about the financial issues? Leta S. Blank, coordinator for the Senior Health Insurance Assistance Program (SHIP) in Montgomery County, Maryland, says that individuals should buy a long-term-care policy only if their annual retirement income is over $50,000 and they have assets of $100,000 to $500,000, not including their home or car. Blank also warns, "Buy long-term-care insurance only if you can afford it without making a lifestyle change and if you have the ability to afford a 20 percent to 50 percent increase in premiums in future years."

But what are the chances that you will ever go to a nursing home, or, if you do enter a nursing home, that you will spend much time there? According to AARP, research suggests that about half of today's older people will spend some time in a nursing home—from as little as a few weeks to as much as five years. AARP cites several factors that could increase your chances of going to a nursing home:

- You live alone or have no relatives who could care for you at home.

- Your family members tend to live into their eighties or older.

- Your family has a history of heart problems, high blood pressure, diabetes, or some other serious or chronic health problem.

- Your family has a history of stroke or of Alzheimer's or Parkinson's disease.

If, after considering all these factors, you decide to buy a long-term-care policy, be prepared to do some hard work to get the right policy from the right company. You'll certainly need to shop around, which means interviewing salespeople from several companies and being steadfast in your refusal to sign anything until you've completed your comparisons. Do not buy any policy that you don't completely understand. People who buy policies get a 30-day "free look" during which they can return the policy and get a refund.

BEYOND THE NURSING HOME: OTHER OPTIONS

Until a few years ago, a nursing home was about the only place in town where you could place an elderly parent or spouse who was no longer physically or mentally able to live in her own home. That situation has changed dramatically. Today, in most areas of the country, there are many more options, including group homes, assisted-living facilities, and continuing-care retirement communities. The growth of these facilities has been prompted by the recognition by both nonprofit organizations and entrepreneurs that there is a serious and growing demand for services for the elderly. In addition, many people who are reaching their sixties and seventies want to prepare for the day when they can no longer live independently.

It is also clear that not all elderly people need a nursing home, with its skilled 24-hour care or even its long-term custodial care. Instead, many people can get by with help just in preparing meals, dressing, bathing, or some of the other activities of daily living. American entrepreneurs, always quick to spot a business opportunity, foresaw that as the U.S. population grew older, millions of elderly persons would need that kind of help. Thus was born a new assisted-living industry. Currently, about 750,000 Americans live in more than 31,000 assisted-living facilities, according to the National Center for Assisted Living's 2012 State Regulatory Review.

The trend has also resulted in the creation of thousands of continuing-care retirement communities—often called CCRCs— where you can move in while you are still in good health, and later, if your health deteriorates, move to higher levels of care until you finally reach the nursing home level. One word of caution about CCRCs, though: be prepared for a case of "sticker shock" when you see the cost of some of these facilities.

I talked with Karen Love, founder and board treasurer of the Consumer Consortium Advancing Person-Centered Living, about the growth and challenges facing the assisted-living industry. "The assisted-living industry has grown phenomenally in the past two decades," she told me. "There are approximately three-quarters of a million residents living in assisted living. Compare this to the estimated 1.6 million nursing home residents, an industry that has been around significantly longer than assisted living, and one understands the explosive growth experienced in assisted living." Current economic conditions, she noted, have slowed the growth and development of assisted-living residences.

"There are a number of significant challenges facing assisted living: developing more options to make assisted living available to low- to moderate-income individuals; ensuring that person-centered care, seen as the gold standard, is the norm; and addressing the direct-care workforce crisis." While baby boomers have been the driving force behind finding alternative means of long-term care other than nursing homes, Love added, "They will also be a driving force behind reshaping quality care and services to support the often physically frail and cognitively impaired resident population of assisted living."

Choosing an Alzheimer's Facility

When a loved one develops Alzheimer's disease and requires full-time care, you may be left with little choice but to find a facility that specializes in dementia cases. As I mentioned at the beginning of this chapter, this was the task I was faced with when my wife, Sara, became ill. With the help of my three grown children, I chose a group home where she would have 24-hour care. But moving her from our home to an unfamiliar place and leaving her in the hands of strangers was the most traumatic event of my life.

There is, of course, no way to prepare for an emotional decision of this magnitude. But, in retrospect, searching for a place for Sara would have been somewhat easier if I had known more about Alzheimer's and about the senior-care industry.

Many different types of facilities provide care for Alzheimer's patients. They include:

- Large *nursing homes* and *assisted-living homes* with special floors or wings for early-stage and late-stage "memory" patients.

- Medium-size *assisted-living* facilities with different levels of care. Some residents need only moderate amounts of care with their daily activities. Residents with Alzheimer's disease or Parkinson's disease will need more intensive care.

- *Group homes,* often converted residences with small staffs, caring for up to 15 late-stage Alzheimer's or other patients.

The prices for Alzheimer's care vary widely, as I mentioned earlier. In the Washington, DC, metropolitan area, prices range from $7,000 to $12,000 a month for the more luxurious places and $3,000 to $4,000 a month for the smaller, less elaborate facilities. Prices in other parts of the country will be different. When looking at such facilities, it is important to find out what kind of programs—music, art, exercise, singing—are being provided to help keep patients alert and entertained.

So, where do you begin your search for an Alzheimer's facility?

Thanks to the Internet, a Google search will turn up the websites for Alzheimer's facilities in almost any part of the country. For instance, www.Retirement-Living.com will bring you to the Retirement Living SourceBook, which lists hundreds of senior facilities in the Washington, DC–Maryland–Virginia region. Similarly, www.seniorhomes.com will give you listings for facilities in Chicago and in cities around the country.

Taking the time to do this research will give you an overview of what is out there, the type of care available, and the cost of various residential treatment centers. Indeed, it may lead you to the conclusion that you can't afford the care you would like to provide for your loved one. If you have long-term-care insurance, that will help you pay the bills. If you don't, you may have to rely on relatives or friends to help you take care of your loved one at home.

Even if you do your Internet search efficiently, you may be overwhelmed by the number of choices available. So I would suggest getting help from a professional geriatric-care manager who knows the Alzheimer's facilities in your area and who has helped other people find homes for family members. Once again, the Internet will come to your aid. Go to the website of the National Association of Professional Geriatric Care Managers, www.caremanager.org Then, click on "Find a Care Manager" and insert your zip code, and you will get a list of local care managers. In your initial conversation with the managers, ask their fees and the amount of time they would need.

At some point, you will want to inspect the homes that are on your "possible" list. But before you go, think carefully about the things you want to look for and the questions you want to ask.

I talked about this process with Georgia Weiss, the president of Avalon Assisted Living Facilities, based in Bethesda, Maryland. Her company manages two group homes in suburban Maryland, including the home in which my wife, Sara, resides, and nine group homes in suburban Virginia. Weiss has worked in the field of geriatric patient care for many years. She earned a master's degree in social work at Boston College in 1976, when Alzheimer's was still called "senile dementia." Her courses included an emphasis on gerontology, which was then emerging as a new field of study and treatment for the elderly.

In the years that followed, Weiss worked in various senior facilities. In 1997, she decided to open her own business and began to acquire and equip small group homes in suburban Virginia, where the limit is 8 patients; the limit in Maryland is 15. Many of the patients in Weiss's homes have either advanced memory loss or physical problems, or both. When selecting her staff, Weiss said she looks for individuals who are "patient, caring, and have a reverence for the elderly." The temperament and the abilities of the staff members, she said, "are absolutely critical to the success of each home."

Weiss said she chose to open small group homes because "people who have more advanced memory loss do much better in a smaller, homelike environment where there is a high level of personalized care in a familylike atmosphere." The small group home, Weiss continued, "is the best option available for these patients compared to the larger, more institutionalized places, which are too overwhelming for them."

On the other hand, Weiss added, the larger facilities may be more helpful to patients with early-stage Alzheimer's who can still communicate well and can take advantage of the entertainment and other activities that are offered.

I asked Weiss what people should look for when selecting a facility for a loved one.

"When you walk in, your initial reaction should be: is the place clean?" she replied. "If they can't get that right, you have to wonder what else is going wrong."

"Is the place clean?" sounds like a simple question. But for Weiss, who has spent her career working in senior facilities, that question quickly subdivides into other questions, such as:

- When you enter the home, does it smell clean?

- Are the patients dressed, and do they look and smell clean?

- Do the members of the staff look neat and clean?

- Are the bathrooms clean?

- Are the beds made? Are the rooms neat?

- Do the trash cans look as if they have been emptied?

Obviously, on a brief visit to a group home or a larger assisted-living facility, it is difficult to get to know very much about the place. However, since most such facilities are regulated by state or local governments and undergo frequent inspections, you can probably find out what the inspectors said about the home. You may also want to see the reports by fire marshals and other safety officers. Increasingly, it is also worth asking what a home has in the way of standby generators that can provide emergency power if the electric service in the area or region is disrupted by violent storms. The aged and ailing patients in senior facilities, large and small, are very vulnerable when the lights go out and the heat or air conditioning is shut off for extended periods, as was the case in July 2012.

But I discovered that the best way to find out what is going on in a home is to talk to the relatives of patients, especially relatives who visited frequently. They will tell you what they see and hear and how they feel about the care that their loved one is getting. They will also tell you how well or badly they interact with the staff. Their observations will help you make a decision about whether you want to bring your wife, husband, father, or mother to that home to be cared for. In those circumstances, you need all the help you can get.

The Continuing-Care Option

Before Sara's illness, the most attractive option for us at our stage of life was a continuing-care retirement community, or CCRC for short. A CCRC provides both housing and access to healthcare at three levels:

- *Independent living.* You live in your own cottage or apartment for as long as you are physically and mentally able to.

- *Assisted living.* If, as time passes, you require help with dressing, bathing, eating, or any other activities, you can move to the assisted-living area or receive the services you need in your home.

- *Skilled nursing care.* If you require skilled nursing care, you can move to a residence that provides specific care that is part of your CCRC.

To get a sense of what a CCRC is like, Sara and I visited the pastoral 130-acre Asbury Methodist Village in Gaithersburg, Maryland. I also talked with Douglas W. Leidig, chief operating officer of Asbury Communities, Inc.

Asbury Communities, a nonprofit corporation, supports several not-for-profit continuing-care retirement communities: the Asbury Methodist Village campus in Gaithersburg; Asbury-Solomons Island in Solomons, Maryland; Bethany Village in Mechanicsburg, Pennsylvania; Inverness Village in Tulsa, Oklahoma; and Springhill in Erie, Pennsylvania. It also supports the Asbury Foundation, a 501(c)(3) organization that secures support to enhance the quality of life for seniors served by the Asbury system of communities.

Asbury Methodist Village, founded in 1926 as a home for retired Methodists, has grown into a community with more than 1,300 residents. Asbury is open to all, regardless of sex, creed, color, religion, or national origin.

Like many CCRCs, Asbury offers its residents a sense of security because they know that if they become ill temporarily or need long-term care as they age, it will be available in familiar surroundings. Moreover, Asbury's managers provide residents with opportunities for an active physical and intellectual life. Residents can take part in a variety of programs and use the community's recreational facilities.

Asbury and most other CCRCs require both entry fees and monthly fees. If we had wanted to move to Asbury, the managers would have studied our financial assets and monthly incomes to see whether we could afford to live there for an extended period of time. Our costs would have depended largely on the kind of housing we selected. To move there, we'd first have had to sign a contract that spelled out the details of what we'd pay and what we'd get in return. The contract would also have told us what additional costs we could expect if we had to move to assisted living or to the nursing home.

Retired couples often come to Asbury after selling their homes and using the proceeds to pay the entrance fee for a single-family villa or an apartment.

In 2011, the standard entrance fee for a courtyard manor home (new product) ranged from $495,000 to $650,000, and that for a villa ranged from $456,000 to $475,000. For an apartment, the 2011 entry fee ranged from $46,350 to $356,500.

The monthly fees for 2011 were as follows:

- Villas ranged from $901 to $1,717 with no second-person fee.

- Courtyard homes didn't have a range for 2011; they were all at $1,650 with no second-person fee.

- Original apartments (Mund, Trott, and Edwards-Fisher buildings) ranged from $1,495 to $3,327 with a second-person fee of $644.

- Diamond apartments ranged from $1,973 to $3,212 with a second-person fee of $644.

- Wallace Building apartments ranged from $2,455 to $2,724 with a second-person fee of $644.

- Park view apartments ranged from $2,050 to $2,784 with a second-person fee of $133.

In addition to the villas, courtyard homes, and apartments, there are other apartments—called Kindley at Asbury Methodist Village—for people who need assisted living.

There are no entry fees for persons who enter Asbury from the outside community and go directly into assisted living. However, the monthly fees are 5 to 17 percent higher than for those who move from independent living to assisted living. Monthly fees in assisted living are tied to the level of care required, of which there are three.

Daily rates for the three levels of care for nonsubscribers* (paid monthly) are:

Level 1 $221.00
Level 2 $276.00
Level 3 $321.00

---

* A subscriber is a person who has paid an entrance fee; a nonsubscriber is a person who does not pay an entrance fee but enters Asbury in need of assisted-living care.

There is a one-time $300 administrative fee and a $75 phone setup charge.

Daily rates for the three levels of care for a couple (again paid monthly) are:

Level 1 and Level 1	$321.00
Level 1 and Level 2	$376.00
Level 1 and Level 3	$424.00
Level 2 and Level 2	$431.00
Level 2 and Level 3	$479.00
Level 3 and Level 3	$527.00

Daily rates for the three levels of care for subscribers* (paid monthly) are:

Level 1	$190
Level 2	$245
Level 3	$307

There is also a $75 phone setup charge.

Daily rates for the three levels of care for a couple (also paid monthly) are:

Level 1 and Level 1	$258
Level 1 and Level 2	$314
Level 1 and Level 3	$376
Level 2 and Level 2	$368
Level 2 and Level 3	$431
Level 3 and Level 3	$495

There is also a $75 phone setup charge.

The villa or apartment entrance fee does not offer any equity ownership in a villa or apartment. However, it is possible to get a refund of one's entrance fee under certain circumstances. An incoming resident has three choices: the standard entrance fee plan, a 90 percent refundable plan, and a 100 percent refundable plan. The prices of these latter two plans are higher than those of the standard entrance fee plan. No interest is paid on the entrance fee under any plan.

As of 2011, 65 percent of new residents chose the standard entry fee plan; the other residents were typically split between the 90 and 100 percent refundable plan options.

Asbury officials point out that this financial structure has many benefits. "Although you are paying a significant sum as a 'down payment' up front, the monthly fees throughout the remainder of one's time at the community are significantly lower than they otherwise would be for a comparable rental property, especially when you take into account all the benefits and services that are included," one said.

"In addition, in a 'down economy' such as we have encountered post-2008, the buying power of community living is a welcome 'economy of scale' that helps individuals to fight inflation and realize additional value for their retirement dollar.

"Finally," the officials said, "Asbury provides a 'care assurance' benefit, which means that even if residents outlive their financial resources (through no fault of their own), Asbury's Foundation raises funds to pick up the financial slack, and residents have never been asked to leave the community for their inability to pay the monthly fees."

Asbury is one of many CCRCs in the Washington area. Each one is different. Housing, recreational facilities, entrance fees, monthly charges, and contracts all vary. People in the CCRC business like to say, "When you've seen one CCRC, you've seen one CCRC."

If you're interested in a CCRC, the best advice is to shop around. If you want to move into a CCRC, consult a lawyer before you sign any contract.

CCRC contracts generally fall into three categories, all of which include housing and residential services, but which differ in the amount of healthcare they cover and in how you pay for accommodations, services, and healthcare. Here are some definitions:

- An "extensive" or "A-type" contract provides for the pre-payment of healthcare expenses in a manner similar to an insurance arrangement; it is sometimes known as a "life-care agreement." Extensive agreements offer the most health-related services for one predetermined monthly fee that does not change if there is an increase in the level of care received by the resident.

- The "modified" or "B-type" contract includes a specified amount of long-term healthcare in the monthly fee. Additional healthcare beyond the prepaid amount is available on a fee-for-service basis.

- The "fee-for-service" or "C-type" contract does not include long-term healthcare in its monthly fee. While residents receive priority in admission to the assisted-living and skilled-nursing-care facilities, they pay the full daily rate for the applicable level of care.

Asbury Methodist Village is a C-type, or fee-for-service, organization. If Sara and I were residents of Asbury and had to receive skilled nursing care, it would cost us from $306 to $493 a day, depending on the level of care we needed. However, our long-term-care policy would pay only $110 a day for me and $140 a day for Sara. If and when we ran out of money, we probably would be eligible for Maryland's Medicaid program, which covers the cost of room and board and skilled-nursing-care services. Items such as private-duty nurses, hair appointments, and so on are not included in Medicaid-covered expenses. In the Asbury system, 35 percent of nursing home residents are on Medicaid.

The Asbury Foundation annually provides funding support for benevolent care and other capital and special programs. More than $3 million in new gifts and pledges was contributed to the Asbury Foundation in 2011. Across the Asbury system of communities, more than $1.1 million in benevolent-care assistance helped 46 independent-living and assisted-living residents who had outlived their resources. In addition, Asbury provided $7 million in uncompensated services to those residents who are on Medicaid.

That generosity is in keeping with the long-established tradition at Asbury that the organization does not ask residents to leave because they cannot afford to stay there, said Douglas W. Leidig, Asbury's chief operating officer.

The financial reality of operating Asbury, Leidig noted, is that the organization's income from monthly fees doesn't always cover its expenses. What keeps Asbury going, he said, are the entrance fees, the ability to invest that money, and the charitable donations that the foundation receives. The income earned from investments and the donations for care assurance help cover operating expenses.

It all makes sense, of course. But it also makes me wish that we had saved more money during our working years.

For More Information

The following organizations can provide information on home care, assisted-living facilities, small group homes, nursing homes, and continuing-care retirement communities:

Consumers who are interested in learning more about CCRCs can contact the Commission on Accreditation of Rehabilitation Facilities (CARF)–Continuing Care Accreditation Commission

(CCAC). CARF-CCAC is the major accrediting body for CCRCs in the United States. Phone: 1-866-888-1122. Its website, www.carf.org, offers a consumer guide to CCRCs.

Consumers who are interested in learning more about long-term-care insurance, investment, or financial planning products can visit www.ArthurSteinFinancial.com.

The Assisted Living Federation of America (703-894-1805) offers a free package of consumer information, including the *Guide to Choosing an Assisted Living Residence*. The group's website is www.alfa.org.

The National Association for Home Care and Hospice offers an online guide to choosing a home-care provider, as well as other consumer information. Its website is www.nahc.org.

The American Health Care Association represents long-term-care and assisted-living providers. For free information on long-term healthcare options, call 202-842-4444. The group's website is www.ahcancal.org.

The Consumer Consortium Advancing Person-Centered Living (CCAL) publishes a booklet titled *Choosing an Assisted Living Facility: Considerations for Making the Right Decision*. The booklet costs $12.95. A purchase form is available at CCAL's website, www.ccal.org. To order by phone, call 732-212-9036.

The National Association of Professional Geriatric Care Managers helps families coordinate care for parents or spouses who need medical treatment or assistance with daily tasks. Fees vary. The organization's website is www.caremanager.org. For information, call 520-881-8008.

A number of organizations provide information on long-term-care insurance and suggestions on how to shop for policies:

The Senior Health Insurance Assistance Program (SHIP) has counselors in many communities across the country who can offer advice on Medicare, Medicaid, Medigap, and long-term-care insurance. Phone numbers of local counselors are listed in the back of the printed booklet *Medicare and You 2013*, which is sent to most Medicare recipients. The information also is available at http://www.medicare.gov/Contacts/; click the button, "Help & Resources," then click "Publications" in the left column.

The General Services Administration's Federal Citizens Information Center publishes a free *Guide to Long-Term Care Insurance* prepared by America's Health Insurance Plans (AHIP). The guide is available at http://publications.usa.gov/USAPubs.php or by phone at 1-888-878-3256.

LTCfeds.com. This is the website for the Federal Long Term Care Insurance Program (FLTCIP), a federal program created for federal employees and retirees in 2000. This site contains extensive information on the subject of long-term-care insurance.

www.Leadingage.org. Leading Age (formerly AAHSA), a non-profit organization represents 5,600 not-for-profit nursing homes, assisted-living residences, continuing-care communities, and independent living, home, and community-based services and adult day services for the elderly.

www.naic.org. National Association of Insurance Commissioners (NAIC) is the organization of insurance regulators for the 50 states. The states regulators' primary responsibility is to protect the interests of insurance consumers. Be sure to check out the Shoppers Guide to Long-Term-Care Insurance.

Where Do I Want to Live After I Retire?

The question of where to live after you retire can have a certain *Fantasy Island* quality. It's easy to imagine yourself retiring and moving to that fabulous vacation spot where you spent two weeks soaking up the sun and scuba diving. Wouldn't it be great fun to live there full-time?

Or perhaps you can see yourself moving to that great little town in the West where you went to college. If you lived there, you could wake up in the morning and look at the mountains where you love to hike. And you could take some of those history courses you didn't have time for when you were in school. What a pleasant life that would be!

Over the years, Sara and I have watched many of our friends and relatives pursue their retirement dreams by packing up and moving to places where they found a better climate, a more interesting lifestyle, or a lower cost of living. Often, I've noticed, these retirement moves are determined by the whereabouts of family members. Many of the people who live in our retirement community came here from distant places because they have children and grandchildren who live nearby. They moved to be closer to them.

Surely, one of the lessons of growing older is that when you are in your retirement years, it's highly desirable to be close to your family. Because illness is always a possibility, you never know when you might need help. It might be help with simple things, like getting to a doctor's appointment or going to the supermarket. Or, on a more serious note, it might be the help and comfort of having family members nearby when you go into the hospital for surgery.

Being close to family members has many dimensions, of course. For many retirees, including me, the opportunity to spend time with their children, and especially with their grandchildren, can be the best part of retirement. I like to think it is rewarding for the grandchildren as well. Even so, a discussion of retirees who move—or who don't move—always comes down to this old idea: "Different strokes for different folks." The decision to move or to stay is very much an individual matter, and each retiree has to make his own decision as to where to go—or whether to go at all.

Our Florida Investigation

A year after I retired, Sara and I thought seriously about leaving the Washington, DC, area and moving to Florida. There were at least a couple of good reasons to make the move: we would get away from the ice and snow of Washington winters, and we would be closer to many of our relatives and friends who live in the Sunshine State, including Sara's four sisters.

But there were also several good reasons to stay. We had lived in the Washington area for more than 25 years. Our children and grandchildren were all nearby, and so were the doctors and dentists that we'd used for many years. We also felt very much at home. We had become attached to the city's great monuments and cultural attractions, and we liked the small communities of suburban Maryland and Virginia.

The idea of moving also raised several hard questions. First, were we ready to put forth the physical and psychological effort that moving requires? Only a few years earlier, we had sold our big five-bedroom house and moved to a small two-bedroom apartment in our retirement community. The memory of that move was fresh in our minds, and I, for one, wasn't sure I was ready for another move.

Second, what would it cost us to move to south Florida? Where would we live? How much would we have to spend for housing? And how would the cost of living in Florida compare with the cost of living in the Washington area?

These are the kinds of questions that face all retirees who are thinking of moving, whether they're considering the Sunbelt areas of the country, such as Florida and Arizona, or the newly popular retirement communities of the West and Pacific Northwest. One thing is sure: no matter where you want to go after you retire, choosing a place to live requires a considerable amount of research. Frankly, the process is pretty much the same whether you are heading north, south, east, or west.

Sara and I did some in-depth research when we were thinking of moving to south Florida. The process would have been the same if we had been going to any other area of the country. You could easily repeat this type of research for any destination that interests you. In any event, this is what we did.

We took a trip to south Florida and spent three weeks in Broward County and Palm Beach County, where we made a fairly intensive effort to get to know the local communities. Although the weather in the region can be unpredictable at times, we were there during a period of warmth and sunshine.

Clearly, Florida's biggest drawing card is a pleasant climate during the winter months. In mid-February, I swam and played golf under blue skies and bright sunshine, with temperatures in the eighties. I wore short-sleeve shirts and shorts on days when my friends at home were dressed in parkas and using their snow shovels to dig out from under a big storm.

In the course of our visit, Sara and I tried to get a sense of what it would be like to live in Florida full-time. I was particularly interested in whether it would be cheaper to live in Florida than in the high-priced Washington area. Cost was important to us, as it probably will be to you, because, like many retirees, Sara and I were trying to make our retirement dollars last as long as possible.

CHEAPER HOUSING, SMALLER TAX BILLS

To get a line on the cost of housing in south Florida, we visited several new housing developments. We studied and compared prices and the quality of the housing being offered. We also tried to find out as much as we could about the local communities and the facilities and services that were available to residents.

We talked with friends and relatives about their housing experiences in south Florida. At the time, it seemed clear to me that housing in south Florida was much less expensive than housing in the Washington, DC, area. A few years later, when the national housing boom began, home prices in Florida rose rapidly, as did prices everywhere else. Then, when the housing boom went bust, Florida homeowners suffered, as home prices fell sharply and the state racked up a large number of foreclosures. At this point in mid-2012, an accurate comparison of housing costs in Florida versus costs in other states will have to wait until both the economy and the housing market recover.

During our trip to Florida, I asked a former Maryland neighbor, Walter Packer of Boynton Beach, about the cost of food in Florida compared to that in Maryland. Packer, who had spent 25 years in the grocery business, had a keen eye for food prices and quality. Packer said at the time that he found that fruits and vegetables in Florida were 20 percent cheaper and groceries generally 10 to 15 percent cheaper than in Maryland. Restaurant meals in Florida also tended to be less costly, Packer said, especially during "early bird" seating hours, which usually started around 5 p.m. or 5:30 p.m. These reduced-price meals are so popular that the "early bird" has been jokingly dubbed the state bird of Florida.

When I looked at the price of clothing in Florida, it seemed to be about the same as in Maryland. But we wouldn't need winter wardrobes, although we would need additional summer clothes. Then there was the matter of how much it would cost us to relocate. I was sure that it would cost several thousand dollars, but at that point I had not yet tried to come up with a firm figure.

When I got home from south Florida, I continued my research by phone and found that if we moved, we would save quite a bit of money on taxes. That was chiefly because Florida, unlike Maryland, Virginia, and the District of Columbia, has no state income taxes. That could mean a significant saving for us, since we are residents of Maryland. I knew how much I paid each year in Maryland taxes, but as a journalist, I was curious about how much retired couples living in the DC area paid in state taxes.

I asked certified public accountant and tax expert William A. Fritz, Jr., of Fritz & Co. in Fairfax City, Virginia, to help me figure it out. We made these assumptions: the couples were over

65 and had annual taxable income (before taxes, the standard deduction, and exemptions) of $77,000, with $30,000 coming from Social Security, $42,000 from pensions, and $5,000 from interest on investments.

Based on 2011 state income tax rates, if the couples take the standard deductions, Bill Fritz said, they would pay state income taxes of $1,332 in Maryland based on the maximum locality rate and assuming that the income is allocated 50 percent each between the couple. The District state income tax would be $1,978, and the tax in Virginia would be $547. By moving to Florida, the couples would save those amounts. Maryland offers a pension exclusion, which is reduced by the amount of Social Security benefits received.

In the District, a maximum pension exclusion of up to $3,000 a year is available for District and federal government pensions. This could result in a tax reduction of up to $180 a year per person, but it was not factored into these calculations.

The Virginia tax is considerably lower, Fritz told me, because the state grants a $12,000 "age deduction" for individuals over 65. Thus, a Virginia couple could get a $24,000 deduction. However, this age deduction phases out at certain income levels for individuals born after January 2, 1939. Single taxpayers lose $1 of the deduction for every $1 that their adjusted federal adjusted gross income (AFAGI) exceeds $50,000. For married couples, the dollar-for-dollar loss begins when their AFAGI exceeds $75,000.

In recent years, the tax picture in Florida has improved for anyone who was thinking of moving to the Sunshine State, according to Martin R. Glickstein, a certified public accountant in Maitland, Florida. First, the Florida intangible tax was repealed in 2006. Second, in 2008, Florida increased the state's homestead exemption from $25,000 to $50,000.

The intangible tax was a tax on an individual's total investments, including stocks, bonds, mutual funds, and money market funds. The state did not count bank deposits, certificates of deposit, annuities, U.S. government obligations, Florida state or municipal bonds, or retirement accounts such as 401(k) or Keogh plans. Intangible taxes remain in effect on mortgages taken out in Florida.

Meanwhile, legal residents of Florida have seen an improvement in the homestead exemption on their personal residences. This feature reduces the assessed valuation of a house by up to $50,000, which, in turn, reduces the homeowner's tax bill. The first $25,000 reduction applies to all property taxes, including school district taxes. The second $25,000 reduction applies to the assessed value between $50,000 and $75,000 and only to nonschool taxes.

With regard to general sales taxes in the Washington region compared to Florida, this is how they stack up. Maryland and the District are both at 6 percent. In addition, both Maryland and DC exempt groceries, prescription drugs, and over-the-counter medications. Virginia's sales tax is 5 percent; however, groceries are taxed at 2.5 percent, and prescriptions are exempt. The Florida sales tax is 6 percent. However, some counties in Florida add sales tax surcharges of up to 1.5 percent.

MOVING AND ADJUSTING

As Sara and I mulled over the idea of moving to Florida, we talked about the process of adjusting to a new state and a new community. We realized that if we moved, we'd have to adjust not only to a new climate, but to a new home, a new geography, new cities and towns, new highways, new newspapers and TV stations, new libraries, new businesses, and new customs. For instance, when I was visiting Florida, I couldn't find a bank that was open on Saturdays, and that was rather annoying.

Of course, before we moved, we would have to sell our apartment in Maryland, buy a new home or apartment in Florida, and then furnish it. That would be a guaranteed hassle that would discourage me but probably not Sara. She was a very good organizer, and she had handled our last move quite efficiently.

As I mentioned, we had sold the house we had lived in for 25 years and moved five miles away to our present condominium apartment in a high-rise building. But I can easily remember the feeling of loss when we left the old neighborhood, with its familiar faces and shopkeepers who called us by our first names. And I can also remember the strangeness of getting used to a new home in new surroundings, even though we hadn't moved a great distance.

One possible alternative to a full-fledged move was to become a "snowbird"—someone who goes south in the winter and north in the summer. That is what some of our friends and relatives did. They bought small and relatively inexpensive apartments in Florida, often fully furnished, that they use for three or four months during the winter. But they keep their homes in the Northeast and thus do not have to deal with Florida weather in the summer.

That would mean finding the money for a second home. If we could do so, the arrangement would have many advantages. We'd be close to our children and grandchildren in the North most of the year. Indeed, they'd probably insist on coming to Florida to visit us during their winter holidays! We'd also be close to our Florida relatives for several months—long enough to enjoy their company, but not long enough to wear out our welcome.

Sara, however, was dubious about having two homes to worry about. Not only would it be a financial strain, she said, but she feared that problems could arise in either home when we were away at the other. So we slowly dropped the idea of having two homes.

That left us with only one option: a full-time move to Florida. Several neighbors had recently done that, and they reported that things had worked out well for them. While we were weighing the pros and cons of making the big move, several other factors began to dominate our thinking and eventually persuaded us to stay in the Washington area. Those factors involved our children and, especially, our grandchildren.

When I discussed relocating in one of my *Washington Post* columns, I received a dozen letters from readers offering their opinions. One of the most persuasive letters came from a woman who told us about her mother's move to Florida.

Although her mother came north to visit occasionally, the daughter said, her mother missed seeing her grandchildren grow up and in many ways had lost touch with her daughter's family.

The message in the letter was clear: don't do it. The more we talked about moving, the more we came back to the question of whether a move would cause us to lose touch with our young grandchildren. We kept thinking of that old saying, "Out of sight, out of mind."

But there was one other important factor: if the time came when one of us became seriously ill, we did not want to be living in Florida, far from our children. That would force our kids to fly to Florida to deal with our health problems.

Sara and I had been through that experience with my parents, who were occasional snowbirds. When my father became ill, Sara and I went to Florida to bring them back to our home. When Sara's brother became seriously ill, his son spent many weeks commuting between New York and Florida. We had seen many other examples of that kind of situation.

Finally, when we weighed all our reasons for moving against all our reasons for staying, we decided to stay.

Choosing a Place to Live

When Sara and I thought about moving, we considered going to Florida because of its climate and its cost-of-living advantages.

It was also where many of our friends and relatives lived. We felt that if we were going to make a major move at a late stage of our lives, it would be reassuring to be close to family and friends.

But wherever you may want to go to retire, you are likely to face the same kinds of questions and dilemmas that we faced. Also, choosing a retirement community is no easy task. Ask David Savageau. For nearly three decades, this Denver native has been studying and writing about the best retirement communities in America. He is the author of *Retirement Places Rated*, 7th edition (Wiley, 2007), a 302-page book that profiles 200 retirement areas across the United States and rates them in terms of their ambience, living costs, climate, services, personal safety, work opportunities, and housing.

When I came across Savageau's book, I was awed by the extraordinary amount of research that had gone into its creation. As a reporter who has spent his life gathering information, I could appreciate the effort involved. So I was anxious to meet Savageau and get his thoughts about why retirees do or do not move and why some moves are successful and others are not.

Savageau has traveled extensively in the United States and has visited nearly every one of the 200 areas he has written about. In the course of his wanderings with his wife, Karyl, and a silver Airstream trailer in tow, he has had an opportunity to talk to many retirees about their relocation experiences, both good and bad. Savageau says that people who are thinking about relocating should begin to plan their move long before they retire. "The decision to relocate should require at least five years in advance of the official day of retirement," he observes.

There is a well-established process that many people use to prepare for a retirement move, according to Savageau. Commonly, they spend vacations, both short and long, in an area that they find attractive. In time, they may acquire a second home in the area, spending more and more time there in order to see whether they would be comfortable living there year round.

People need sufficient time, Savageau points out, to develop "a sense of place." Some people, he notes, make the mistake of simply moving to Florida or Arizona without doing any homework. When they find that they don't like the hot summers or the traffic congestion or other aspects of those areas, they move again and again until they wind up back where they started, saying, "There's no place like home."

Despite all the talk about moving, Savageau says, U.S. Census Bureau figures usually show that less than 5 percent of people over 60 moved between states over the past two decades. Since 2008, however, relocating for retirement has dropped because of the slowing economy and the difficulty of selling homes. There is a positive side to the slump, though. Home prices have fallen most sharply in the traditional retirement states of California, Nevada, Arizona, and Florida, and some careful shopping can uncover sale or rental bargains.

Renting in a new destination, Savageau says, is a great way to "rehearse retirement" without making a long-term financial commitment. In some locations, landlords prefer older tenants because of their good credit scores, stability, and "ownership virtues," that is, taking care of their home. Resorts and college towns offer the widest choices for apartment, home, and condominium rentals.

When he first began studying mobility patterns nearly 30 years ago, Savageau says, climate was the main reason that retirees moved, and almost all the movement was to the Sunbelt states. While climate is still a factor today, he notes, cost of living is now the major reason for relocation. The desire to save money prompts many retirees to go to less expensive communities where housing is cheaper and taxes are lower. Another factor that is rising in importance is interesting opportunities for part-time or seasonal work.

Retirees also are expanding their range of destinations, with the Pacific Northwest, the Rocky Mountains, and New England becoming popular relocation choices. Savageau has counted 42 states that are now seeing newcomers. Indeed, he says, before you move to any retirement community, find out whether you are likely to be welcomed by local residents. If the community is not hospitable to newcomers, you may not want to move there.

Places that are used to seeing and welcoming newcomers include college towns, areas near military bases, and vacation and resort areas. Lately, a small trend has started among suburbanites who prefer to downsize but don't want to leave a familiar area—so they retire downtown, perhaps to a former hotel or department store that's been converted to condominiums. In all of those places, Savageau suggests, retirees are likely to find it relatively easy to make new friends. Making new friends and developing a satisfying social life are vital to any successful relocation, he says.

Trying to Find Friends Fast

I know what Savageau is talking about. Although Sara and I did not move to Florida, we did move locally to a brand-new 300-family apartment complex in a retirement community. We found ourselves among a diverse group of people who had one main thing in common: they were all new residents. And they all wanted to make friends fast.

This was our third such experience. On two previous occasions, we had moved to new single-family housing developments where, each time, everybody in the neighborhood was new, and they too all wanted to make friends fast. What happens in these circumstances is a lot like the Great Land Rush. Your phone begins to ring with calls from your new neighbors, and your mailbox is soon stuffed with invitations for cocktails, brunch, and dinner. Then the games begin. It may be poker, bridge, canasta, or mah-jongg. After that, you begin to get invitations to join a club: the Lions, the Kiwanis, Rotary, the Knights of Columbus, the American Legion, and so on.

Then you hear from the fun bunch. "We're going to the water-walking class on Wednesdays. Would you like to join us?" Or, "We need a few more singers in our little theater group. We're doing *The Mikado*. Won't you come down and try out?" That's how it all begins. You can probably guess how most of these overtures will end.

At the cocktail party, your new neighbors all seemed as if they'd rather be someplace else, except for the guy in the corner. You spent most of the evening listening to him talk about his gallbladder surgery. His story took longer than the operation.

At the dinner party, the food was good. But the other three couples all seemed to know one another from their old neighborhood, so they spent most of the evening talking about people and places they all knew. None of it meant anything to you.

At the brunch, you met an interesting couple, and it seemed as if you could be friends. The only problem was that they spent most of their time on cruises. In fact, they were heading out the next morning on their forty-third cruise. It didn't seem that they'd have much time to spend with you.

You joined the poker game and played for about six weeks, but you quit because one of the players complained constantly about his bad luck. So you made an excuse about working late and left. The canasta game also broke up about a month after it began, because two of the players said the other two players were too slow.

Friends were easier to find at the service clubs and the fraternal organizations. And although you didn't get a singing role in *The Mikado*, it was fun helping with the costumes, and you became friendly with several people who, coincidentally, had joined the water-walking class. So you joined, too.

In any event, a couple of years after we moved to each of our new communities, we had a whole new set of friends. Of course, they didn't include any of the people we had met when we first arrived. We found friends in our own way and at our own pace.

That outcome is very much in keeping with research findings gathered by Cathy Goodwin, an independent career and business consultant living in Seattle, Washington. Goodwin is the author of *Making the Big Move* (New Harbinger Publications, 1999). Although it is out of print, the book is available at some booksellers and at http://www.RelocationStrategy.com. Goodwin has lived all over North America, from Connecticut to California and from Alaska to Florida. Having moved frequently, she has developed a keen sense of what it takes to adjust to life in a new community.

Goodwin is a strong believer in the take-it-slow approach. All too often, she says, new arrivals rush to get involved in community activities and make new friends. "There's a real tendency to charge in and say, 'I want to feel at home right away.'" But that's not the way to go, she adds. "It takes two years at a minimum to feel at home in a new place."

Goodwin suggests that people wait a while before trying to make new friends or getting involved with volunteer activities. She reasons as follows: the people you initially become friendly with when you move in are unlikely to still be your friends by the time your second year rolls around. By then, you probably will have found friends you like better. But it may be difficult for you to get away from some of your earlier acquaintances.

The same rule applies when it comes to volunteering for community activities, Goodwin says. It's a good idea to wait until you become familiar with the volunteer opportunities that are available. Some volunteer jobs will be far more interesting than others. "When you're new, you don't know what the good stuff is." And if you don't wait long enough to find out, she adds, you could lock yourself into activities that might be hard to get out of.

Of course, if you don't move, you won't have to worry about finding new friends. But many retirees do move, and for good reasons. And the evidence is that they find communities and friends that they enjoy and are happy that they made the move. It can be done. Just look before you leap.

For More Information

Brady, Barbara. *Make the Right Move Now: Your Personal Relocation Guide*. Asheville, NC: B.M. Brady, 2007.

Howells, John. *Where to Retire: America's Best and Most Affordable Places*, 7th ed. Guilford, CT: Globe Pequot Press, 2011.

Velazquez, Jodi. *Slick Move Guide: Secrets You Need to Know If You Are Moving*. Oakdale, PA: Knepper Press, 2007.

How Should I Arrange My Estate to Save on Taxes and Avoid Probate?

Living in a retirement village has many advantages: no grass to mow, no leaves to rake, and no snow to shovel. It also has some drawbacks, one of which is that we live among a large group of elderly people. Thus, it is not unusual for us to hear that one of our neighbors has died. While we are sad to hear such news, we are not surprised. The people who live in this community are in their sixties, seventies, or eighties. Some of them are even in their nineties. And while most of the people we know lead active, busy lives, we are aware that sooner or later the aging process will take its toll.

For Sara and me, the deaths of neighbors are reminders of our own physical vulnerabilities. Indeed, the memory of our medical experiences has focused our attention on whether we were properly prepared for the day—hopefully, far off—when one or both of us would die.

We have discovered that in this complicated world, death is not only an emotional event, but also a legal event and even a taxable one. A favorable outcome depends on advance planning, getting good advice, and carefully assembling your financial records and documents.

The decision to organize our financial and family affairs did not come easily. Like most people, we weren't eager to think about dying. And we had even less incentive to think about wills and trusts and estate taxes, subjects that ordinarily would make our eyes glaze over. But Sara and I talked it over and decided that whether we liked it or not, one of these days we would have to depart. That being the case, we wanted to do what we could to achieve three goals. First, we wanted to depart in a neat and orderly way, creating the least amount of stress for our children. Second, we wanted to make sure that our heirs would get what we wanted them to get. Third, we wanted our estate to be settled with the smallest possible tax bill and the least amount of hassle.

To do all that, we got some good advice and made a series of decisions that will, we believe, accomplish those goals. Our guide through this legal jungle was Rhonda J. Macdonald, an attorney and certified public accountant whose office is in Vienna, Virginia. Macdonald is a specialist in wills, trusts, and other estate-planning matters.

I think it is fair to say that the process we went through in making our estate-planning decisions was a learning experience. Sara and I both learned many things that we had never known before about what the law requires and the opportunities that the law offers. And as a journalist writing about retirement-related matters, I learned things from other experts in estate planning that were both useful and surprising. In the course of this chapter, I will try to convey an understanding of what Sara and I did and what we learned.

It goes without saying that the experience of creating an estate plan did not make me, in any sense, an expert on the subject. The story of what we did is merely that and no more. It is certainly not a complete guide to estate planning. In fact, many aspects of estate planning are not even mentioned here, because we did not deal with them. Thus, if and when you focus on this aspect of retirement, you may have a very different experience from the one we had.

Planning Ahead

The first thing that Sara and I did, even before we talked with Macdonald, was to arrange our funerals. We have a family burial plot, so we know where we're going to be laid to rest. By making the arrangements with a funeral home in advance, we were able to negotiate the price and lock it in. This means that there will be no additional charges, even if our funerals take place years from now. Also, we'll be able to pay for the cost over the next several years. All this means that our children won't have to rush around making funeral arrangements in a crisis atmosphere. I've seen that happen to other people, and it's an unhappy sight.

But planning for your funeral is not—pardon the pun—the end of the story. Unfortunately, you also have to get ready for what happens before you die. Often, that involves a period of illness that may require its own kind of preparation.

When Sara and I met with Macdonald for the first time, we talked about what would happen if either of us became so seriously ill that we could no longer make our own decisions about our medical treatment. Macdonald recommended that we sign a document called an *advance medical directive*. In my case, it allowed me to name Sara as the single individual who could make all my healthcare decisions for me if I were physically or mentally unable to make them myself. It also allowed me to name an alternative person if Sara were not available.

Medical directives, Macdonald said, vary by state. Some states have a medical power of attorney, and others a living will. In Virginia, where Macdonald is based, both types of medical directives have been combined into a single document called an advance medical directive. The main purpose of my own advance medical directive is to make it clear that I do not want my doctors to keep me on life-support equipment or procedures if they decide that I have a terminal condition or that I am in a "persistent coma" from which there is no reasonable possibility of recovery. I want them to understand that if one of those situations occurs, I would prefer to die naturally. Since I would be unable to tell that to my doctors directly, I also make it clear that I am relying on the document itself to be "the final expression of my legal right to refuse medical or surgical treatment."

While the wording of my document fully expresses my wishes and my hope that the doctors will follow those wishes, it isn't quite that simple. Macdonald explained that in virtually every hospital, there is an ethics or other committee that makes the final decision on whether to "pull the plug" on a patient for whom there is no hope of recovery. That may take some time if the patient shows even the smallest sign of life.

In my advance medical directive, it says that before any life-ending action can be taken, a medical team must decide whether I am able to make my own healthcare decisions. This determination is to be made by my physician, along with a second physician or a clinical psychologist. After they examine me, they must submit a report in writing. Until they do, they can't withhold or withdraw treatment.

What role did my wife play in all this? As mentioned, in my directive, I gave her the power to make all my healthcare decisions for me if I were unable to make them myself. These could be trivial decisions about my reactions to medication or far-reaching decisions about terminating my life. She was, in fact, authorized to make almost any medical decision for me, and she even had the power to direct the writing of a "no code" or "do not resuscitate" order. (Incidentally, when Sara signed her advance medical directive, she named me as her representative and gave me similar powers.)

Because Macdonald has her office in Virginia, the advance medical directive that we signed is a Virginia version. Macdonald noted that these directives vary from state to state, but added, "My experience, happily, has been that a living will validly executed in any state is honored in another state."

A Matter of Trust

On more than one occasion over the years, Sara and I have watched friends and relatives try to deal with one of life's most difficult problems: the mental incapacitation of a spouse or parent because of a stroke or the swift onset of Alzheimer's disease. When that happens, especially in the event of a stroke, the stricken individual may suddenly lose his ability to make informed legal and financial decisions. What is needed, therefore, is a way to appoint a spouse or child to make those decisions for the person who is ill. The way to do that, Macdonald told us, is to sign a general durable power of attorney, a document that allowed Sara and me to appoint each other to act for the other in the event that either one of us could no longer make our own financial and legal decisions. In a way, the durable power of attorney resembled our advance medical directives, except that the durable power of attorney deals with financial matters rather than health matters.

The powers granted in a durable power of attorney are extremely broad. In essence, Sara and I gave each other almost complete power over the financial side of our lives. For instance, my power of attorney allows my wife to gain access to my bank accounts, to manage or even sell my real estate, to sell or transfer my investments, and more. And, of course, Sara has given me the same powers.

While these powers are sweeping, Macdonald said, they often are needed in a hurry when a spouse becomes mentally incapacitated. Even so, she said, the original document should be kept in a safe place from which it will not be removed until the person who signed it becomes incapacitated. Macdonald cautioned us that such documents become effective immediately when you sign them, not just when you become ill. She said she tells clients that they need to have a high level of trust in the person to whom they give their power of attorney. In other words, make sure you really trust each other.

Those Sweetheart Wills

At this point, Sara and I were feeling somewhat self-satisfied with our progress. We'd been able to make advance funeral plans, and we'd managed to understand and sign two complicated legal documents: advance medical directives and powers of attorney. But as we soon discovered, that was only the beginning of our learning experience in estate planning. We still had a long way to go.

Essentially, we were taking a quick course in wills, trusts, and estate taxes. Macdonald was a patient instructor, always willing to explain an obscure concept over and over again until we understood it. And there was a great deal to understand. Estate planning is an extremely complicated field, especially for a person who is not a lawyer and can't even do his own tax return. But thanks to Macdonald, I finally began to understand that estate planning has many advantages.

Macdonald says that married people who come to see her often bring her what she calls "sweetheart wills." That's the kind of will in which the husband leaves everything to his wife and the wife leaves everything to her husband. Indeed, that's the kind of will that Sara and I each had before we began to work with Macdonald.

Here's how sweetheart wills work: if I die, I can leave everything I own to Sara tax free, at least from a federal tax viewpoint. The problem arises when she dies. At that point, the total dollar value of her estate, less any available federal and state estate tax exemptions, may be subject to estate taxes. Thus, while a sweetheart will is romantic, it may not keep Uncle Sam or your home state from taking a bite out of your estate after the second spouse dies. Nor will it avoid the expense and delays of going through probate court.

Pursuant to the 2010 Tax Act, which adopted for the first time a "portability election," as discussed later in this chapter, it is possible for a married couple to leave all assets to each other through sweetheart wills without having adverse federal estate tax consequences.

However, generally, a married couple with sweetheart wills runs the risk that after the first spouse dies, the surviving spouse will change her will, diverting an inheritance away from the beneficiaries that both spouses agreed upon while they were living (for example, the couple's children) and leaving the inheritance to new beneficiaries who were not contemplated while both spouses were alive.

The best example of this is that upon remarriage, a widow might want to leave everything to her new spouse, to the exclusion of her and her former husband's children.

Another important factor to consider is that with simple sweetheart wills, a married couple will not have the type of estate-planning documents that make sense in most states. In addition to wills, these documents include revocable trusts (also known as "living trusts"), which have the advantage of being able to avoid the courthouse process known as *probate.*

What is probate? Generally speaking, it's a legal process that is used to wind up a deceased person's financial affairs. It involves required court oversight, filing fees, and, very likely, legal fees.

The personal representative or executor who is named in the will prepares an inventory of the assets and liabilities of the estate, pays any taxes and bills that are due, and makes sure that the heirs get the bequests that have been left to them. However, all of those actions have to be approved or at least reviewed by the court. Many people try to avoid the probate process if they can, because of the time it takes to settle an estate and the filing fees and legal fees involved.

Macdonald told us that the best way to both minimize estate taxes and avoid probate was to create a *revocable living trust* for each spouse, which is used to hold the assets belonging to each. The trust also may contain a *bypass trust,* which before recent changes in the estate law, including the portability election, was necessary in order to reduce or eliminate estate taxes. These trusts are still used for a nontax purpose, which is to guarantee an inheritance for beneficiaries chosen by both spouses rather than leaving this choice to the surviving spouse.

Now, even after we decided to create two living trusts, Sara and I still needed wills. In our wills, we each named a personal representative and specified that representative's duties. Our wills describe how we want our personal property to be distributed and give other instructions for winding up our financial affairs. However, detailed instructions about who inherits what, when, and how are all stated in our trust documents.

By creating two bypass trusts, we were setting the stage so that we could take advantage of each spouse's federal tax exemption. This exemption provides that, during life and/or after death, each spouse can transfer a certain amount of money to children or other beneficiaries without incurring gift or estate taxes.

As mentioned previously, however, the portability election that was adopted for the first time in the 2010 Tax Act now makes it possible to utilize each spouse's federal estate tax exemption without having to have bypass trusts and the retitling of accounts and assets that is associated with bypass trusts.

However, there are other (nontax) consequences of not having bypass trusts (which become irrevocable when the first spouse in a married couple dies). By having bypass trusts, a married couple can guarantee that the ultimate beneficiaries of their estate plan (such as children) will inherit, without having to run the risk of the beneficiaries' inheritance being diverted as a result of a remarriage of the surviving spouse.

THE ESTATE TAX: A STRANGE STORY

As of the publication date of this book, there is no guarantee that the 2010 Tax Act will become permanent, as it is scheduled to expire at the end of 2012. Predicting what will happen with the estate tax in 2013 is made more difficult because 2012, when this book is being written, is an election year, and there is a great deal of uncertainty about what a future Congress will do.

According to Macdonald, either of two scenarios is likely:

1. The $5 million federal estate tax exemption, which is the largest estate tax exemption ever adopted (effective January 1, 2011), will be made permanent, hopefully with the continuance of the indexing for inflation that began on January 1, 2012 (as indexed, that figure for deaths in 2012 is $5.120 million).

2. President Obama's 2013 budget proposes a permanent $3.5 million federal estate tax exemption (this was the estate tax exemption adopted via the 2001 Tax Act, effective for deaths in 2009).

Of course, another option, although by far the least popular, is that Congress will pass yet another temporary estate tax exemption, not a permanent exemption. This would continue the $5 million indexed exemption, but only on a temporary basis.

In addition to raising the federal estate tax exemption to $5 million, the 2010 Tax Act made three other significant changes:

1. It adopted the portability election, as discussed previously in this chapter.

2. The top marginal federal estate tax rate was reduced to 35 percent from the previous 45 percent.

3. The $5 million estate tax exemption was indexed beginning January 1, 2012 (so that for 2012 deaths, the figure is already $5.120 million). The indexing of the estate tax exemption is attractive because it means that the exemption should not become outdated as a result of inflation.

The portability election is considered a tax victory for married couples who prefer to keep things simple and want to leave all their assets to the other after the first of them dies. However, according to Macdonald, it is likely that in adopting this part of the tax law, Congress did not realize that the election is onerous for some couples who otherwise would not have had to file an estate tax return because the portability election is made only upon filing a federal estate tax return.

According to Macdonald, the filing of a federal estate tax return is not an insignificant matter, from the viewpoint of both legal fees and the work required to gather the information, including appraisals, needed to support the details that must be provided in an estate tax return. Macdonald notes that a federal estate tax return is by far the most detailed and complex estate-related tax return that she prepares.

GETTING YOURSELF ORGANIZED

How do you know what your estate is worth? Here's my two-step plan for measuring the value of your estate and organizing your financial information.

Step 1

Take a personal financial inventory by adding up the value of everything you own and everything you owe. If you're married, make three lists. First, list the assets and liabilities that are in your name only; second, list those that are in your spouse's name only; and third, list those that you own jointly. When you're done, subtract what is owed from what is owned on all three lists. That will give you a rough idea of the value of your estate, your spouse's estate, and your shared estate.

Typically, a list of assets will include bank accounts, certificates of deposit, stocks, bonds, and mutual funds. The value of your life insurance should also be listed. Include the fair market value of your home, car, boat, home furnishings, jewelry, real estate, and pension accounts. A list of liabilities will include any money you owe, including your mortgage, bank loans, car loans, and credit card balances.

Step 2

Think for a moment about how hard it would be for your spouse or your children to find all your personal and financial information if you weren't around. You can spare them a lot of grief by doing the job for them. I suggest keeping your information and documents in a place where they are safe and easy to find. A fireproof file cabinet or home safe may be better than a safe-deposit box.

Start by including your will and your trust documents. If you have prearranged your funeral, include the name and phone number of the funeral home, the agreements you signed, and a record of your payments. Among the documents that should be in your file are the deeds to your home and other property that you own, the title to your car, your military discharge and veterans' benefit papers, your marriage license, divorce papers, birth certificates, citizenship papers, passports, and immigration papers. Also, you should include your bank, brokerage, and mutual fund account numbers and the addresses or phone numbers of those institutions, as well as your credit card numbers, balances, and phone numbers. Finally, include your Social Security number, the amount of your monthly payments, and, if you have direct deposit, the name of the bank to which the check is sent. Do the same for pension payments.

Make sure that a family member knows where you keep the key to your safe-deposit box and the name of the bank where the box is located. Make a list of what's in your box. Also, list the names, numbers, and details of all your insurance policies, especially life, auto, and homeowners' policies. And don't forget health-insurance and nursing home policies. Make a list of your doctors and their phone numbers, too. By the way, once you've done all these things, make sure to tell your spouse, your children, or other relatives what you've done and where they can find all the information.

As Sara is fond of saying, "Preparedness is next to godliness."

Thinking About the Unthinkable

Unfortunately, when it comes to deciding what will happen to your money and your property after you die, you can do everything right and still have things come out wrong.

Any lawyer who has practiced estate law for any length of time can tell stories of parents who tried to do the right thing by leaving their money and property to their children in equal shares, believing that the show of fairness would help maintain family harmony after they died. But all too often, it doesn't work out that way.

"When it comes to money, family loyalty goes out the window," I was told by Jeffrey L. Condon, a Santa Monica, California, estate lawyer, who talked about the conflicts that can arise after parents die. The children are not just the parents' children anymore, Condon said, "They're people dividing money." And that often makes them behave differently from the way they would if their parents were still alive.

Condon told the story of a couple who left everything they owned equally to their three children. However, years earlier, they had spent $250,000 to send one son to medical school. Another son had attended a local junior college, and the daughter had not gone to college.

After the parents' death, this discrepancy in education spending caused a rift among the siblings. The doctor's brother and sister felt that he should give them part of his inheritance to equalize what their parents had spent on each of them. The doctor disagreed; he no longer speaks to his siblings.

What the parents should have done, Condon said, was to equalize their spending on their children during their lifetime. Parents who occasionally help a child financially tend to forget about unequal treatment, he said. "But rest assured, your children haven't forgotten. And they're keeping score." Condon and his father, attorney Gerald M. Condon, told the story in their book *Beyond the Grave: The Right Way and the Wrong Way of Leaving Money to Your Children (and Others)*, revised edition (Harper Business, 2001).

Family strife can arise out of many inheritance scenarios. Second marriages, especially those involving widows and widowers with grown children, can be disasters waiting to happen. All too often, inheritances wind up in the wrong hands because of poor planning, failure to use the right legal tools, or just plain greed. Lawyers who specialize in wills, trusts, and estate planning say that there are many ways to create inheritance problems. But there are also ways to prevent them. Here are a few examples.

UNEQUAL SHARES

Parents often tell Rhonda Macdonald that they want to leave more money to one child than to another. Usually, the reason given is that one child is very successful and "doesn't need the money," while the other child is relatively poor. When Macdonald hears that, she tries to convince the parents that it's a bad idea to give unequal shares to their offspring simply for economic reasons. "By leaving a smaller share to your successful child, you are punishing him or her for success. And by leaving a greater share to your poorer child, you're rewarding his or her lack of success," Macdonald tells her clients. That argument seems to work, Macdonald said, and few of her clients wind up leaving their children unequal shares for economic reasons.

SECOND MARRIAGES

The classic horror story begins when Dad dies and Mom remarries. Mom and her second husband each have three grown children. They each really want to leave their individual wealth to their own children, but they have put all their savings and property in both names and thus own everything jointly. That means that if the second husband dies before Mom does, all their joint assets will automatically become Mom's property. It will then be up to Mom, in her will, to decide what his children and her children will get. And even if Mom leaves most of her second husband's assets to his children, they will have to wait until she dies to get their inheritance. That could take a long time, and his kids are likely to make a considerable fuss about the delay.

The easiest way to avoid these conflicts, Macdonald said, is for remarried spouses to keep their assets in their own names. That allows them to leave their individual money and property to their own children through their wills. If they've already put their assets in both names, they can go back and retitle them.

If Mom will need income to live on after her second husband dies, he can set up a trust for her that contains his assets, Macdonald said. Such a trust is called a "qualified terminable interest property," or QTIP, trust. It allows Mom to receive income from her second husband's assets after his death. It can also guarantee that the principal of the trust ultimately will be inherited by the second husband's children, although, once again, they may have to wait until Mom dies.

In some cases, this may not be the complete story. For instance, in Virginia, Maryland, and the District of Columbia, Mom can claim one-third of her second husband's assets if he omits her from his will or leaves her less than one-third of his assets, even if the assets are held in his own name. This privilege can be waived through a premarital agreement.

WATCH OUT FOR THOSE IN-LAWS

Arthur and Mary, a couple in their eighties, plan to leave their estate to their only son, Roger, who is 55. They hope that when he dies, Roger will pass along his inheritance to their grandchildren. But they worry about what will happen if Roger dies before his wife, Selma, does, as she would then get her husband's inheritance. They are not sure that Selma would actually pass the inheritance along to the grandchildren. In fact, if Selma remarries, the inheritance could be passed to her second husband and members of his family, and that's not what the grandparents have in mind.

One way for Arthur and Mary to protect their grandchildren's inheritance, according to Macdonald, is to create a generation-skipping trust, which will ensure that the couple's money goes to their grandchildren when they reach a specified age. Here's how that would work. Their son, Roger, would become the trustee of the trust after the deaths of his mother and father. Roger would get the annual income generated by the trust or a percentage of the value of the trust each year. He could use as much of the principal of the trust as necessary to pay expenses for the health, education, and support of himself and his children.

A generation-skipping trust can have tax advantages. There is a generation-skipping tax exemption equal to the estate tax exemption, which can avoid estate taxation at Roger's death while guaranteeing an inheritance for his children.

That amount would be counted as part of Arthur or Mary's estate when the second spouse dies. Taxes would be paid on the total value of the estate, less the individual estate tax exemption.

WHEN CHILDREN OWE MONEY TO THEIR PARENTS

Anger and confusion are almost inevitable when children borrow money from their parents and don't pay it back. After the parents die, it is often unclear how much was borrowed, when and how the loans were to be repaid, and whether interest was to be charged. Worse yet, with the passage of time, children often start to think of the money that they borrowed not as loans but as gifts. On top of all this confusion, Macdonald said, some of the children are likely to demand that their siblings repay their loans so that the total inheritance is not reduced by the debts.

Macdonald said she tries to head off these problems by asking clients, when they come in to write their wills, to give her the specific details of any loans they have made to their children so that she can include the information in the wills. That way, she said, when the parents die, the terms of the loans will be on record.

NAMING THE EXECUTORS AND TRUSTEES

When parents write their wills and create trusts, they often name their children as personal representatives, executors, or trustees, making them responsible for placing a value on the assets of the estate, distributing the assets to the heirs, and filing various documents, including the deceased's final income tax return. But how many children in a family should be given this task? The answer, says Macdonald, is, "All of them." In Macdonald's experience, the offspring will not be happy if they are left out, no matter where in the world they may be. They will want to be part of any decision affecting their inheritance, be it by phone, fax, or e-mail.

This is particularly true, Macdonald said, because executors and trustees are allowed to charge a fee for the work involved in settling their parents' estate. When there is more than one executor or trustee, the fee is shared. If only some of the children are named as executors and if they opt to receive executors' fees, Macdonald said, that may skew what would otherwise have been an equal division of assets among the children.

GETTING THE BUSINESS

At times, parents flatly refuse to give equal shares of their estate to all their children. One situation in which this often occurs is when there is a family business. On those occasions, Macdonald said, parents may insist on leaving the firm to the offspring who have been working with them in the business for years. That may make the other children in the family unhappy, even though they chose to work in other fields. Indeed, those children might even sue on the grounds that they are getting a smaller inheritance than their siblings. If the parents think that such a lawsuit is likely, Macdonald said, they can attempt to head it off by inserting a "no contest" clause in their wills. Under that clause, if the children sue, they lose the inheritance that they were slated to get. "If they sue, they get nothing," Macdonald said.

DISINHERITING CHILDREN

There are lots of reasons why parents want to omit children from their wills or inheritance plans. The most common one is that a child is estranged and the parents haven't seen her for years; in some instances, the child has been involved with alcohol or drugs or has been in trouble with the law.

Jeffrey and Gerald Condon caution parents that if they omit a child from their will, one of two things is likely to happen: the child will either sue or become a burden to her siblings.

Although such lawsuits generally fail, they can be costly to the other children. In fact, the Condons noted, the other children may find it cheaper to settle than to pay the legal costs involved.

The Condons advise that instead of cutting a child out of their wills, parents should put the child's share of the estate into a trust. They can then specify when and how their estranged son or daughter will get any money or income from the trust. The Condons also recommend that if parents omit a child from their wills, they should write a letter to the child, telling her what they're doing. The letter may encourage the child to renew her ties with the family. At least, they say, it will give the child fair warning of what is going to happen.

TALKING IT OUT

Most lawyers agree that whatever inheritance or estate plan you adopt, it is important for you to explain your actions by discussing them with your children and with other relatives. Children should know exactly what their parents intend to do with their money and other assets. If they have problems with their parents' plans, it's a good idea to let them find that out before it's too late.

For More Information

Here are just a few sources of guidance on wills, trusts, and taxes.

BOOKS

American Bar Association. *The American Bar Association Guide to Wills and Estates*, 3rd ed. New York: Random House, 2009.

Condon, Jeffrey L., and Gerald M. Condon. *Beyond the Grave: The Right Way and the Wrong Way of Leaving Money to Your Children (and Others)*, rev. ed. New York: Harper Business, 2001.

Palermo, Michael T. *AARP Crash Course in Estate Planning* (updated). New York: Sterling, 2008.

Ventura, John. *Kiplinger's Estate Planning*. New York: Kaplan Publishing, 2008.

WEBSITES

National Association of Financial and Estate Planning: www .nafep.com. Click on "Public Information Menu" to navigate a drop-down menu listing "Estate Planning Basics."

Nolo Law for All: www.nolo.com. Click on "Wills, Trusts and Estate Planning."

How Can I Age Successfully?

At some point in our lives, we all have to admit to ourselves that we are getting older. Signs of aging creep up on us in subtle ways. Gray hairs show up when we are in our thirties. We need bifocals in our forties, a hearing aid in our fifties, and a heart bypass operation in our sixties. Then we start to have memory lapses. While they are merely annoying when we are in our younger years, these lapses become scarier as we age.

In a way, even retirement is a sign of aging—not a physical one, perhaps, but an event that is usually related to increasing age. Whether we choose to retire at 62, at 66, or at 70, retirement usually occurs when we have completed about three-quarters of our life span. Thus, when we retire, it is clear that we're moving into the final quarter of our lives.

That is not meant to sound grim. In any football game, the last quarter is often the most exciting. The same can be true of retirement. It is one more chance to add points on the scoreboard of your life. It is, in fact, a very special time of life, as many retirees have discovered. Indeed, in a survey for the National Council on the Aging, 49 percent of Americans aged 65 to 69 said, "These are the best years of my life."

I can relate to that sentiment. The opportunity to write the "Retirement Journal" column after I retired—and its popularity—was the frosting on the cake of my career. Even the chance to put my ideas and experiences together in this book was a long-cherished ambition, realized at age 73 and still enjoyable at 85 as I write these words for the fourth edition. Yes, the clock is ticking. But it can tick for many more years. As retirees, our primary challenge is to stay healthy long enough to enjoy the pleasures and opportunities that retirement can bring us.

Thanks to modern medicine and rising living standards, increases in life expectancy have been dramatic. As noted earlier, a 65-year-old woman can expect to live to 84, while a 65-year-old man can look forward to living until 81. Medical advances are steadily extending those expectations. Living to 100 will soon be commonplace. But what does it take to reach those extended ages? As gerontologists and social scientists learn more about the aging process, they are able to provide us with increasingly better answers to that question.

I found some interesting ideas in a book about growing older, *Successful Aging*, by John W. Rowe and Robert L. Kahn. The book is based on the MacArthur Foundation Study of Aging in America, which took 10 years and cost $15 million. Among other things, the study looked closely at the history and habits of people who were aging well.

The book contains lots of good news for people who are in their sixties and seventies. The MacArthur study exploded many of the myths about aging and showed that, with proper diet, exercise, and medical care, elderly people can remain physically active and mentally alert for many years. Successful aging, the authors say, is based on three characteristics:

- A low risk of disease and disease-related disability
- High mental and physical abilities
- The desire to remain actively engaged with people

While heredity plays a role in longevity, the authors report that individual lifestyle choices and behavior over many years have the most influence on whether one ages well. Better yet, the authors tell us that it is never too late to change one's lifestyle for the better.

The lesson here is quite clear: the best way to prepare for a healthy old age is to adopt a healthy lifestyle while you're young. But even if you didn't do that—I didn't start thinking about my health until I was in my fifties—there's still time.

Confronting Illness

While there are many things we can do to preserve our health during retirement, we can't always avoid illness, which often strikes unexpectedly. I know this both from my own experience and from watching the ebb and flow of life in my retirement community, in which the average age is about 70 or 75. Hardly a month goes by that we don't hear about a friend or neighbor who has suffered a heart attack or a stroke or who has developed cancer.

In fact, I had my own medical battle, as I mentioned briefly in Decision 8. Shortly after I retired, I decided that it was time to get a long-postponed physical checkup. The checkup led to the discovery of several clogged blood vessels in my heart. Although they had been partially cleared by angioplasty 10 years earlier, the blood vessels were now clogged again. My doctors said a four-way heart bypass operation was necessary.

I agreed to have the surgery, but the whole idea of having to undergo a serious operation so soon after I retired seemed truly unfair. I had worked for almost 45 years, and when I finally felt that I was ready to retire, my health and perhaps even my life seemed to be in jeopardy.

The experience of going through open-heart surgery—and its aftermath—forced me to confront my own mortality in a way I had never done before. I wondered how long my retirement might last. And I asked myself, even if I survive, what will be the quality of my life?

Fortunately, I recovered from my surgery within a few months, but the experience left me feeling that if there was any-thing I wanted to do in retirement, I should do it soon. This sense that my life might be limited was intensified by my wife's medical experiences. Three years before my surgery, Sara had undergone breast cancer surgery. She recovered after a nine-month ordeal that included chemotherapy. After her recovery, she decided to retire from her job at GE, where she had spent 22 years. But, unfortunately, Sara continued to have medical problems. A few years later, she was diagnosed with thyroid cancer and underwent surgery to remove her thyroid. She survived that challenge, only to develop dementia, as mentioned in Decision 9.

Thus, Sara and I have spent a considerable amount of time in retirement confronting major medical challenges. Sooner than most retirees, perhaps, we have learned the truth of the old say-ing, "With good health, everything is possible. Without it, nothing is possible."

Pumping Iron

After my heart surgery, my doctor sent me to a nearby cardiac rehabilitation center to improve my physical condition. It was there that I learned both aerobics and weight lifting. The first few weeks were rough, because my muscles were weak and my stamina was limited. But I slowly gained back my strength, and my physical condition improved. I tell my friends, especially those who trade stocks, that exercise is one of the few investments I've ever made that seems to have all upside and no downside.

In fact, until I went to the cardiac center, I didn't understand how easy it is to get hooked on regular exercise. My discovery came about this way: the center was open three days a week—Mondays, Wednesdays, and Fridays. So I would go to the center on those days and work out for about two hours a day. But after about four weeks at the center, I noticed something strange: on Tuesdays and Thursdays, I would wake up feeling restless. I wanted to exercise, but the center was closed. So I began making up my own exercises.

I soon figured out what was happening: exercise had become a habit. When I didn't exercise, my body missed it. Later, I read that natural chemicals called endorphins are released in the body during vigorous exercise. Endorphins can make us feel good and can even produce a feeling of euphoria, sometimes called "runner's high."

I don't know whether other people can get hooked on exercise as easily as I did, but the daily desire to work out made it much easier for me to get out of bed in the morning and go to the exercise room. I never had to fight the feeling of, "Aw, skip it and go back to bed."

After I "graduated" from the cardiac center, I began to work out in the exercise room in our retirement community. The fitness center is located next door to our apartment building. In fact, it is so close that I'd have a hard time thinking of an excuse not to go regularly. Many of my fellow residents also use the exercise room, which was expanded recently because it is so popular. Until I retired, I had no idea that so many retirees devoted part of each day to exercise.

Often, the people who use the exercise room are recuperating from strokes, heart surgery, knee and hip replacements, and other assorted ailments. Others swim laps in the indoor swimming pool. Some do both.

For many residents, walking is the main form of exercise. On any decent day, the sidewalks and paths of my retirement community are crowded with walkers. A popular pastime is "walking the circle," the circle being a 3.2-mile path that goes around the community.

Some of my retired friends are "mall walkers." Each morning, they drive to a nearby indoor mall, walk rapidly around the shopping area for about an hour, and then gather for coffee and gossip. In inclement weather, I often hear the footsteps of the "hall walkers," residents of our building who get their exercise by walking up and down the corridors and steps of our 10-story building. I've done it; it takes about 45 minutes, and it provides vigorous exercise.

Having discovered exercise late in life, I have no illusions about how I look when I'm lifting those dumbbells. When I glance in the wall mirror and see this gray-haired, aging man pumping iron, it's hard to keep from smiling. The sight reminds me of that old magazine ad for bodybuilder Charles Atlas, who boasted that he went from a "97-pound weakling" to "The World's Most Perfectly Developed Man." The ad featured a cartoon of a skinny kid on a beach who loses his girl to a sand-kicking muscleman and resolves to take weight-lifting lessons. As I struggle to lift those weights aloft, I sometimes hear myself saying, as that kid did, "Nobody's going to kick sand in my face!"

Do I wish I had started down the athletic trail 50 years ago? Yes, I do. But it wasn't as though I was a couch potato all my life. As a political reporter and columnist early in my career, I spent years running for campaign planes, trains, and buses. As a homeowner, I spent years mowing lawns, raking leaves, shoveling snow, and painting the house. Sure, it was all work, but it wasn't the kind of regular daily exercise that keeps your muscles toned and your heart healthy. If I had it to do over, I would make more time for exercise, especially because I've learned that exercise is not only good for your muscles but also good for your brain. And what is good for your brain is good for your memory.

That belief, along with the rapid growth of Alzheimer's disease, has evolved into a major national focus on "brain fitness" as people search for the magic key to avoiding the loss of their cognitive functions. The Alzheimer's Association advises people to:

- Stay physically active.

- Adopt a brain-healthy diet.

- Remain socially active.

- Stay mentally active.

Beyond this type of worthy advice, there are numerous commercial firms that offer brain exercises. The jury, it appears, is still out on what approach can prevent or at least delay the devastating effects of Alzheimer's disease.

My Memory and Me

The thing that frightens me most about growing older is the idea that I might lose my memory. Memory is such an integral part of our personalities and our individuality that it is unsettling to see signs that our memories are failing. In fact, not long ago, I began worrying about my memory after several incidents:

- I was shopping at the local mall when I ran into a man I'd worked with for many years, but I simply couldn't remember his name. It was on the tip of my tongue, but

I couldn't dredge it out of my memory. I was embarrassed not to be able to call him by name.

- Another day, I drove to the supermarket, but when I came out, I couldn't remember where I had parked my car. I finally found it after wandering around for several minutes, but I was annoyed with myself.

- While I was at home, I walked from the kitchen into the bedroom to take care of a small chore. But when I got to the bedroom, I couldn't remember why I had gone in there. I had to go back to the kitchen to remember what I wanted to do in the bedroom.

- I took a phone message for my wife from her sister, but I didn't write it down because I was sure I would remember it. When Sara came home and asked if anybody had called, I said no. I had completely forgotten about her sister's call. Hours later, I remembered the call.

- Working at my desk, I found myself trying to recall the name of the capital of California. Once again, it was on the tip of my tongue, but it took a full five minutes before "Sacramento" swam into my consciousness.

After that "memorable" week, I started worrying about my memory. "What's going on here?" I asked myself. "Am I losing my memory? Does this have anything to do with my age?" I took my questions to Marilyn S. Albert, an expert in the field of aging and memory. She was quite reassuring.

"I wouldn't worry," Albert said after I told her about some of my recent memory lapses. Albert suggested a way to tell whether my occasional episodes of forgetfulness were serious or not. She put it this way.

"When you're reminded of the name you forgot or the location of your car and you can say, 'Yes, of course. That's it,' then you are probably fine," she said. "The real time to worry is when you find the name you forgot and you don't get the feeling that you knew it all along." I was happy to hear that, because I think I'm still in the "I knew it all along" camp. That little test also will be good news to my friends and acquaintances. Many people who live in my retirement community, I've noticed, are equally forgetful.

In fact, memory lapses are so common among my peers that they've been given a name. They are called "senior moments." If you listen to the conversations in the lobby, the exercise room, or the local clubhouse, you will hear a resident, in the midst of telling a story, pause and try to remember a name, place, or date. When he can't recall that name, place, or date, the storyteller is likely to remark, "Uh-oh, I'm having a senior moment." It's usually said with some embarrassment, but no one is critical. The listeners simply nod sympathetically. It has happened to them, too.

Remembering people's names, Albert told me, is a common difficulty. "We all forget them," she said. Memory, she noted, is embedded within many connections in the brain. The more such pathways there are, the easier it is to remember a name; the fewer the number of pathways, the harder it is to retrieve that name.

Names are often hard to remember because it is difficult to make an association with a "John" or a "Mary" when it is only a name by itself. To improve one's memory of a John or a Mary, an individual needs additional images or associations that will help create more pathways in the brain.

Albert said that research has shown that there is a link between aging and memory. "We think [the two are] directly related," she said. Memory loss, she added, can be caused by changes in various areas of the brain that result in the loss of nerve cells and the shrinkage of brain tissue. However, Albert also added, "The good news is that we have found that the nerve cells in the cortex are retained." The cortex plays a significant role in memory.

"What seems to be pretty clear is that as people get older, they have more trouble learning new information than younger people," Albert said. In addition, older people may be less inclined to think about cues that might help them remember, say, where they parked their cars—something that younger people do spontaneously.

But older people can overcome these difficulties by working at remembering—for example, by deliberately fixing the location of their car in their mind before they leave the parking lot. Working at the business of remembering, Albert said, is a valuable strategy for older people. The evidence, Albert noted, shows that once older people learn something—and learn it well—"they won't forget it any more rapidly than someone who is younger."

This ability to concentrate, retain information, and recall it, Albert said, is a key measure of the difference between benign and serious memory lapses. "When people are in the early stages of Alzheimer's," she said, "even if they make an extra effort to learn something, they will forget it."

HOW TO HELP YOUR MEMORY

In dealing with my moments of forgetfulness, I've found a number of memory aids and behavioral devices that can reduce the frustration of memory lapses. Here are some of the strategies that I use to get through the day:

- *The calendar.* I use a month-at-a-glance calendar with big boxes, so that there is plenty of room to write down doctors' appointments, social engagements, upcoming birthdays, and the like. Before you make an appointment, make sure to check your calendar to avoid double booking. Then develop the habit of checking your calendar each evening, so that you will know what you have to do the next day, where you are going, and what time you are expected.

- *A place for everything.* If you have trouble finding things like your car or house keys, your watch, or your sunglasses, create a special place for any items that you are likely to need, and make sure that each of those items goes back to its special spot. That way, you'll know exactly where to find your things.

- *Parking your car.* Many shopping center parking lots have numbered lanes or rows. When you park, make a note of your location, and don't hesitate to jot it down. If there is no numbering system, look around, see where you are in relation to the nearest store, and fix that spot in your mind. That way, you'll be able to find your car easily.

- *Things to do.* The single biggest memory aid for both young and old is a list. To remember the things you want to do, make a list. A word of caution, however: one list is useful, but having ten lists only creates confusion. When you develop your list, put the items in order of priority. And confine your list to the things you want to accomplish in the next week or 10 days. Once you've crossed off most of your immediate chores, you can start a new list and repeat the process.

- *Remembering names.* This is a tricky business because we know many people and know them under many different circumstances. For casual first-name greetings with neighbors, I repeat their names to myself until I'm sure I have them fixed in my mind. For family affairs, at which I will see cousins I haven't seen for a long time (and their children, whom I hardly know), I do some serious homework. That often involves making a small chart of the family, the relatives' names, and who belongs to whom. The system usually works—except for my identical twin

241

nephews. I've spent 40 years trying to tell them apart. For a while, only one wore glasses. That helped. But when they both started wearing glasses, I was sunk.

But what did I do about the former coworker I met in the mall, whose name I could not recall? Well, that won't happen again. His name is a lot like that of a famous general, so when I meet him, I'll just think of that general, and I'll be able to come up with his name. As for trying to remember Sacramento, well, sometimes it's easier to look things up than to wait for your memory to supply the information.

- *Keeping your memory in shape.* The best way to do this, the experts say, is to keep yourself in good physical shape. Regular exercise and a proper diet will do as much good for your brain as it will for your muscles. It's also a good idea to keep your mind active, whether you play poker, chess, pool, or the stock market. Reading newspapers, magazines, or novels will help keep those brain cells humming, too.

Aging and Creativity

I was considerably encouraged about growing older after talking with the late Dr. Gene D. Cohen, former director of the Center on Aging, Health and Humanities at George Washington University in Washington, DC. Cohen's view was definitely upbeat. He believed that one's later years can be an extremely creative time of life—intellectually, artistically, and socially. He spelled out his ideas in the book *The Creative Age: Awakening Human Potential in the Second Half of Life.*

Cohen talked about several phases of creativity in later life. Among them were the following.

THE "LIBERATION PHASE"

This is a time, Cohen said, "in which creative expression is shaped by a new degree of personal freedom in retirement or the restructuring of the time commitment to family." When retirees have more free time and comfortable incomes, he related, they often try new things, especially in the field of art. Indeed, he said, the area of folk art is dominated by older people. "For many people," Cohen said, "retirement is like a patron. A patron gives you time to do something other than having to make ends meet."

In the "liberation phase," which Cohen defined as the late fifties to early seventies, people often get a new sense of freedom to speak their minds and to do things that are courageous. Older people have played major roles in world history, Cohen noted. "The greater freedom and courage that many older adults experience," Cohen said, "help explain why a significant number of older adults about or beyond age 70 have assumed the role of 'shapers' or 'shakers' of society." Among those on Cohen's list were Socrates, Copernicus, Galileo, Mahatma Gandhi, Golda Meir, and Nelson Mandela. These movers and shakers fall into what Cohen called social creativity with a "big C," but he also talked about social creativity with a "small c," referring to the opportunities that ordinary people have to do extraordinary things for themselves, their families, or their communities.

THE SUMMING-UP PHASE

This is a time of life, Cohen said, "in which creative expression is shaped by the desire to find larger meaning in the story of our lives and to give in a larger way of the wisdom we have accrued."

"In the role of 'keepers of the culture,'" Cohen said, "the lessons and fortunes of a lifetime are shared through autobiography and personal storytelling, philanthropy, community activism, and volunteerism." Cohen's views should be quite encouraging to anyone approaching his sixties, seventies, or eighties.

REDEFINING OLD AGE

"The picture of late life itself has changed. It is no longer a portrait of passivity, senility, and sexlessness. Today it has become one of activity, vigor, and intellectual robustness." That quote is from Dr. Robert N. Butler, the late president of the International Longevity Center USA, which is affiliated with the Mount Sinai School of Medicine in New York. In a speech, Butler said that he foresaw a time when many people will live to 100 or beyond, will work until they are 90, and will routinely have multiple careers.

A leader in the fields of gerontology and geriatrics, Butler was the first director of the National Institute on Aging of the National Institutes of Health, from 1975 to 1982. In 1976, he won a Pulitzer Prize for his book *Why Survive? Being Old in America*. "This is the first time in human history that the prospect of living a long, healthy, and productive life has become reality for the majority of people in most parts of the world. What was the privilege of the few has become the destiny of many," Butler said.

When I talked with Butler, who died in 2010, he told me of his great interest in seeing how many older people are busy working either for pay or as volunteers, caring for grandchildren, taking part in physical-fitness programs, and traveling. This national surge of activity, Butler said, is part of "a redefinition of what later life is all about."

No doubt, this redefinition will continue. There are 35 million Americans who are over 65, and 5,000 more turn 65 each day. And the baby boomers are now coming down the road. They, too, will give retirement a new meaning.

The Dos and Don'ts of Growing Older

I have always believed that if something is worth doing, it is worth doing well. Golf, for instance, is much more fun when your drives are straight and your putting is accurate. If it takes a few lessons to help you get there—well, it's worth the cost. You can say the same for almost any other endeavor, including growing older. In fact, it is not hard to imagine the day when "retirement schools" become as popular as golfing schools. Until then, learning to age gracefully will remain a do-it-yourself business.

As I grow older, and as I watch the behavior of friends and acquaintances of my age, I find myself making lists of the dos and don'ts of growing older. Together, I believe, they form a strategy that can help you age successfully and gracefully. They have worked and are working for me. Hopefully, they will work for you, too.

THE DON'TS

- Don't bore your friends and relatives by going on and on about your health problems. In fact, when somebody asks, "How are you?"—don't tell her.

- Don't tell the same story to the same person more than once. When you repeat your stories over and over, people think you're getting fuzzy.

- Don't neglect old friends, especially the ones who were an important part of your life. Time goes by quickly, and you don't know how many more chances you'll have to visit with those friends.

- Don't let anger rule your life. Avoid confrontation. It's an imperfect world, and people make mistakes, even when they're trying to do their best.

245

- Don't assume that age makes you wise and that the world is waiting for your advice. If your friends or relatives want your advice, they'll ask for it.

- Don't live in the past. The past may be where you are most comfortable, but it's the present that most people—especially your children and grandchildren—really care about.

- Don't miss your opportunities. You wanted to see a baseball game last year, but you never called for tickets. You wanted to see the new art museum in town, but you never got there. Ask yourself, if you don't do those things now, when will you do them?

- Don't become a grumpy old man. Cheerful is better. Laugh, and the world will laugh with you. Grump, and you'll grump alone.

- Don't annoy your friends and relatives by not dealing with your problems. If you need a hearing aid, get a hearing aid, so that you're not always saying, "What?"

- Don't gripe about your birthdays. Enjoy them. Each year is a gift. Growing old is not a right; it's a privilege. Take a lesson from composer and pianist Eubie Blake, who lived to be 100 years old. "If I'd known I was gonna live this long," Blake said, "I'd have taken better care of myself."

THE DOS

- Do choose a retirement activity that you really enjoy. It can be a part-time job, working as a volunteer, a hobby, or even a sport. Make that activity the focus of your life. It's wonderful to be able to spend time doing something that you really like.

- Do exercise regularly. It's good for the body, but it's also good for the mind. Exercise helps reduce tension and anxiety and provides a sense of physical well-being.

- Do eat healthfully. Information on good nutrition is all around us. Figure out what foods are best for you, and include them in your daily diet. If you're confused, ask your doctor for advice.

- Do stay tuned into the world around you. It's important that you stay mentally alert. Newspapers, books, magazines, and TV shows can keep you up to date on the issues of the day. Think about joining a book club. If you don't have a computer, buy one and get on the Internet.

- Do try to meet new people and develop new friendships. A good way to do that is to join a charitable, religious, or civic group. Volunteers are always welcome.

- Do maintain your physical and mental independence. As long as your health and finances allow, try to handle your own affairs, do things for yourself, and live by your own schedule.

- Do take advantage of your experience and inner strength when personal or family troubles arise. Remember that you've spent a lifetime learning survival strategies. Use your knowledge to help yourself and others.

- Do pace yourself as you age. It's okay to walk a bit more slowly, take more time to go through the supermarket checkout line, and even drive in the slow lane. If other drivers honk at you, let them rush on by.

- Do keep your sense of humor. Make a small mental list of jokes you can tell to friends. As the *Reader's Digest* says, laughter is the best medicine.

- Do find a way to be friends with your children and grand-children, even though they are very busy. You need them, and whether they realize it or not, they need you.

For More Information

BOOKS

Cohen, Gene. *The Creative Age: Awakening Human Potential in the Second Half of Life*. New York: Avon Books/HarperCollins, 2000.

Cohen, Gene. *The Mature Mind: The Positive Power of the Aging Brain*. New York: Paw Prints, 2010.

Hayflick, Leonard. *How and Why We Age*. New York: Ballantine Books, 1996.

Rowe, John W., and Robert L. Kahn. *Successful Aging*. New York: Dell Publishing/Random House, 1999.

WEBSITES

AARP: www.aarp.org. AARP's "Internet Resources on Aging" (www.aarp.org/internetresources/) contains links to many other websites, including those related to specific diseases.

Access America for Seniors: www.seniors.gov. This is a federal interagency website that offers consumer information from dozens of federal and state agencies.

Administration on Aging: www.aoa.gov. This site provides information from the federal agency that deals with issues affecting older Americans.

Alzeheimer's Association: www.alz.org. This site has a wealth of information.

Elder Web: www.elderweb.com. This site provides sources of information for professionals and family caregivers.

Elderhostel: www.roadscholar.org. This describes educational and travel programs for seniors at home and abroad.

National Institute on Aging: www.nih.gov/nia/. The latest news on federal research into aging and other age-related activities can be found here.

SeniorNet: www.seniornet.org. Founded in 1986, this organization provides computer training for older Americans at centers around the country.

Senior Sites: www.seniorsites.com. This site contains a listing of nonprofit providers of senior housing, healthcare, and services.

Index

About the Author

Stan Hinden wrote the "Retirement Journal" column in the *Washington Post* for seven years after his retirement in 1996. *How to Retire Happy* was inspired by this long-running column, which discussed the decisions, dilemmas, and challenges that confront retirees and those who are planning to retire.

The "Retirement Journal" columns were inspired, in turn, by the experiences, good and bad, that Stan and his wife, Sara, had as retirees. Stan's column appeared each month in the Sunday business section of the *Washington Post* from 1997 to 2004. In 1998, the *Post* nominated "Retirement Journal" for the Pulitzer Prize in Commentary. At the same time, the column won an award from the American University School of Communication and the Investment Company Institute for "excellence in personal finance reporting."

Stan has appeared on radio and television and has spoken often on the subject of "What I Wish I Had Known About Retirement." Before he retired from the *Post* in 1996, he spent 12 years writing about stocks and mutual funds in the business section. In total, he spent 23 years at the *Post* as a full-time writer and editor during his 45-year career in journalism. Currently, Stan writes the "Social Security Mailbox" column for the online *AARP Bulletin*, www.AARP.org/bulletin.

Stan was born in New York City on January 27, 1927. He graduated from Syracuse University in 1950 after serving in the U.S. Army during World War II. Stan and Sara Hinden live in suburban Maryland. They have three children, four grandchildren, and three great-grandchildren.

For more information, go to: www.StanHinden.com.